What people are saying about …

BRAVE IS THE
NEW BEAUTIFUL

"In *Brave Is the New Beautiful*, Lee Blum invites you to join a girls' club of a new kind: one that encourages each member to move beyond the shallow waters of insecurity and strive toward a place of depth, courage, and authenticity."

Gwen Smith, cofounder of Girlfriends in God and
author of *I Want It All* and *Broken into Beautiful*

"Bravery looks different on all of us. Maybe for you, bravery is facing your fears so you can step out in faith. Maybe for someone else, it's the willingness to give others access to her story or the courage to leave a job that props up her identity. We all have mountains to climb and giants to face, but we never go it alone. Jesus is with us, and bravery originates from him. He continually calls us upward and onward. If you're in a season of life where you need a new brand of courage and a deeper sense of God's faithfulness, read Lee's beautiful new book. You'll be reminded afresh that you are not alone and that you get to be a work in progress, without the condemnation. Isn't that the best news ever? We're cheering for you!"

Susie Larson, national speaker, talk radio
host, and author of *Your Powerful Prayers*

"All of us strive to be beautiful, but even on days when the image in the mirror shines, we still don't feel pretty because of the pain, shame, hurt, and loss we carry inside. Lee Wolfe Blum shares women's stories, including her own, to peel back the layers. This book is a beautiful representation of the hope that follows the compassion, care, and bravery of sharing our stories. A worthy read!"

Tricia Goyer, author of more than sixty books, including *Life, In Spite of Me* with Kristen Jane Anderson

"'The notion that anyone's life is easy is a mirage,'" wrote Lee. This is a timely message for all who need reminding that our most enduring beauty often lies just beneath the surface of our brokenness."

Constance Rhodes, founder and CEO of FINDINGbalance and author of *Life Inside the "Thin" Cage*

"In *Brave Is the New Beautiful*, Blum deftly dismantles the barriers that keep us from being our true selves—from being vulnerable and real with others. Without clichés and with real impact, Blum reminds us that life is messy and that we need one another. You will find yourself in these pages, and you will find your friends. And you will find your unique courage."

Shayne Moore, founder of Redbud Writers Guild and author

"Though age has eroded my addiction to the culture of youth and beauty, I still sigh for wrinkle-free skin from time to time. Lee

Blum has nailed the healthy alternative for women of any age: courage to go deeper. Her heroines are women who rose above disfiguring accidents, who tore themselves away from destructive relationships, who endured the death or illness of a child. I especially resonated with the chapter on reinvention, a path I have traveled and highly recommend. Read this book and be inspired to find your own brave beauty."

Carolyn Miller Parr, MA, JD, retired judge
and coauthor of *In the Secret Service*

"Lee Wolfe Blum helps her readers understand that courage is not denying, coping, or white-knuckling it but is accepting our brokenness as a gateway to joy. She skillfully guides us through narratives of loss, disappointment, and pain so that we might develop a more authentic faith and become the beautifully brave women God created us to be."

Dorothy Littell Greco, author of
Making Marriage Beautiful

"In this refreshing and beautiful book, Lee guides readers to embrace their authentic selves, noting that it's not as easy as it sounds and takes tremendous courage. Full of first-hand experience and dozens of anecdotes, Lee paints a vision for how powerful women can be when they embrace life fully and freely."

Kirsten Haglund, community relations
specialist at Timberline Knolls Treatment
Center and Miss America 2008

Finding the Courage
to Be the Real You

BRAVE

is the new

beautiful

LEE WOLFE BLUM

David C Cook®
transforming lives together

BRAVE IS THE NEW BEAUTIFUL
Published by David C Cook
4050 Lee Vance Drive
Colorado Springs, CO 80918 U.S.A.

David C Cook U.K., Kingsway Communications
Eastbourne, East Sussex BN23 6NT, England

The graphic circle C logo is a registered trademark of David C Cook.

The website addresses recommended throughout this book are offered as a
resource to you. These websites are not intended in any way to be or imply an
endorsement on the part of David C Cook, nor do we vouch for their content.

Details in some stories have been changed to protect
the identities of the persons involved.

Unless otherwise noted, all Scripture quotations are taken from the *Holy Bible*,
New Living Translation, copyright © 1996, 2007 by Tyndale House Foundation.
Used by permission of Tyndale House Publishers, Inc., Carol Stream, Illinois
60188. All rights reserved. Scripture quotations marked THE MESSAGE are taken
from THE MESSAGE. Copyright © by Eugene H. Peterson 1993, 2002. Used
by permission of Tyndale House Publishers, Inc; NIV are taken from the Holy
Bible, NEW INTERNATIONAL VERSION®, NIV®. Copyright © 1973,
2011 by Biblica, Inc.® Used by permission. All rights reserved worldwide. NEW
INTERNATIONAL VERSION® and NIV® are registered trademarks of Biblica,
Inc. Use of either trademark for the offering of goods or services requires the prior
written consent of Biblica, Inc; NKJV are taken from the New King James Version®.
Copyright © 1982 by Thomas Nelson. Used by permission. All rights reserved.

LCCN 2016954686
ISBN 978-1-4347-1030-7
eISBN 978-1-4347-1038-3

© 2017 Lee Wolfe Blum

The Team: Alice Crider, Erin Healy, Amy Konyndyk,
Nick Lee, Abby DeBenedittis, Susan Murdock
Cover Design: Emily Weigel, Faceout Studio
Cover Photo: Stocksy and Shutterstock

Printed in the United States of America
First Edition 2017

1 2 3 4 5 6 7 8 9 10

To the brave and beautiful women in this world: may we know them; may we raise them; may we be them.

Be kind, for everyone you meet is fighting a
battle you know nothing about.

Wendy Mass, *The Candymakers*

CONTENTS

FOREWORD

No, God! Please don't ask me to tell THAT story!

I'd shared the sexual skeletons in my closet through the Every Woman's Battle series, but they paled in comparison to *this* horrid secret.

I had killed someone by my own negligence, because of my own vanity.

I was a sixteen-year-old junior in high school, driving to my first-period class. I'd driven fewer than two miles from our country home when I remembered that I hadn't yet put on lipstick. As I adjusted the rearview mirror and quickly applied the lipstick, my car jolted. Hard. *Really hard.* My first thought was that maybe I'd hit a farm animal. But I had a sinking feeling it was much worse.

That feeling was confirmed when I ran back to the point of impact and discovered a curly-headed woman lying facedown in the grass next to a mangled bicycle. *I was the one who did this to her.* The realization almost took me to my knees. I desperately wanted to bolt and pretend it didn't happen, but I knew it was entirely up to me to get this woman the emergency help she needed. I ran toward the nearest house as fast as my jelly sandals allowed, but no one was home and the door was locked. So I ran back to my car, drove to the next nearest house, and frantically dialed 911.

A whopping forty-five minutes passed before an ambulance finally arrived. But looking right past me, the paramedic coldly explained, "I'm sorry, but you'll have to call a funeral home. There is nothing we can do here."

That was August 27, 1984. Her name was Marjorie Jarstfer, and her grieving husband, Gary, soon proved to be the bravest, most beautiful image bearer of God that I've ever encountered. He invited me over the night before Marjorie's funeral to tell me about her life and their work as missionaries with Wycliffe Bible Translators. After holding me oh so tight for the longest time and letting me cry all over his flannel shirt, he sat me down in the bay window of their living room, where I gazed hollow-eyed at numerous family photos displayed on a nearby table. I saw how lovely Marjorie was, how much in love she and Gary must have been, and how they obviously were very proud of the family they'd created together. As hard as this was for me, I could only imagine how much harder all of this had to be on Gary and their three adult children.

Gary explained how Marjorie considered herself the bride of Christ and how there was no limit to how much Marjorie loved the Lord. He even elaborated that she had such a close relationship with God that she'd actually sensed lately that he would be calling her home soon. *Yeah, I know. Unimaginable!* Gary then expressed his belief that I had been chosen by God to usher Marjorie into heaven because he knew I'd be strong enough to handle it. I didn't feel strong at all at the time. I was absolutely leveled and flabbergasted at the strength Gary was trying so hard to impart to me. I couldn't wrap my brain around such unconditional love and mercy.

I still can't wrap my brain around it.

As the next several years unfolded, I was invited to funerals, weddings, baby dedications, and Jarstfer family gatherings. To this day, Marjorie's children call me "sister" and her grandchildren call me "Aunt Shannon." I was not only forgiven by this family, but *adopted.*

As a result of this family's lavish love, my image of God was gradually transformed—from a distant disciplinarian to a big, burly middle-aged man in a flannel shirt, ready to scoop me up in a warm embrace and let me cry all over his shoulder, no matter how deeply I'd hurt him.

So how could I *not* share "our story"? I simply had to. No question.

Together, Gary and I were interviewed by almost every major Christian media outlet. Speaking invitations came pouring in, including a couple for Women of Faith conferences. We were so blessed to be able to share the story with so many. This also miraculously opened the door to minister to several others who questioned whether they could possibly survive the guilt of what they'd done. Such as the teenage boy who didn't tie the rappelling knots tight enough to support his best friend. The babysitter who turned her back on the baby she was bathing in the tub when the phone rang. The pastor's wife who accidentally ran over a woman and her dog one foggy night. No one ever asks to join the I Accidentally Killed Someone Club. But it is a comfort to know that you're not the only member. And if other members can learn to live with the guilt and remorse, perhaps there's a thread of hope to hold on to.

The truth is, no matter what we've experienced in life—death, divorce, disease, devastation of *any* kind—there's always someone who has suffered similar wounds. And when "we can comfort those … with the comfort we ourselves receive from God" (2 Cor. 1:4 NIV), something truly supernatural takes place. We simultaneously learn and teach the four most powerful words in the English language—*you are not alone.*

Isn't that what we all should strive to reveal to the world around us—that we are *not* alone in our struggles, our strife, our disillusionments, our disappointments? That we can hobble wounded and emotionally bloodied through life's battles, yet still cultivate the courage to *let our stories matter!* Our life experiences most certainly matter, especially when we bravely use them for God's glory and for the comfort and encouragement of his people.

When Alice Crider, an editor at David C Cook, told me about the concept of Lee Wolfe Blum's book, my heart did a backflip. *Brave Is the New Beautiful.* The title alone had me! Then I learned that Lee would be boldly unpacking various inspiring stories, including her own journey from barely surviving to thriving, and that she would be helping readers cultivate courage to share their own tragedy-to-triumph experiences. Some of these stories don't necessarily have "happily ever after" or "wrap it up with a pretty bow" type of endings. But the lessons gleaned certainly plant seeds of hope deep in the fertile soil of the human heart. I was ready to write a resounding endorsement based on the concept alone.

Then Lee asked if I'd be willing to mentor her through my B.L.A.S.T. program and help her with the launch of this book. I was absolutely elated, especially when I read the complete manuscript. I devoured it (and believe me, you will too) and quickly caught the vision that this book has the potential to start a whole new spiritual and emotional revolution! Why? Because vulnerability breeds vulnerability. Bravery breeds bravery. Beauty breeds beauty. Lee has done a tremendous job of inspiring genuine vulnerability, selfless bravery, and stunning beauty within these pages you're about to encounter.

Yes, you read that right … this book isn't just something you *read*. It is something you truly *experience*. It will be a magnificent encounter with something real and raw, something holy and sacred.

So if you want to leave a lasting legacy of being someone who changes the world through her own willingness to be vulnerable, who encourages others to be their bravest selves, and who radiates irresistible beauty because she brings out the beauty in others, then read on with great anticipation of what God can first do *in* you and then as a result *through* you.

Shannon Ethridge, MA
B.L.A.S.T. coach and bestselling author

One

SHRINKING

She is brave and strong and broken all at once.
Anna Funder, *Stasiland*

This is my moment. I have finally made it. I have arrived. Dana, a super-hip staff member at my church, stands on the large stage with a piece of paper in her hand and prepares to introduce me to a sizable audience of women.

The room is alive with flickering candles. Women are seated at round tables, eager to be inspired. I sit among them, waiting for my call to the stage, my stomach tight and anxious, my armpits perspiring. Despite changing my outfit three times, I've chosen a sweater too warm for this event.

I've dreamed about speaking here, at my home church, this church, where I whispered prayers for years in the wooden pews. Where I sat crying over miscarriages and funerals, and where I now watch my children perform in the annual Christmas play.

My church.

Dana introduces me and stumbles over my name. As she continues, staring at her paper, it sounds like she is reading the details on the back of a shampoo bottle—without glasses. She mumbles something about me having written a book. The crowd welcomes me with obligatory applause.

So much for arriving.

Have I expected too much? Maybe. I remind myself that I'm not the main speaker. She's the one sitting next to me, another author named Sharon, whom they flew in from Colorado. She's the one they advertised, the crowd-pleaser, the reason all these women bought tickets. I'm just the warm-up.

I suck in a breath, and despite my shaking knees, I walk up to speak. I appear relaxed on stage, and the audience even laughs at the right parts. My talk is brief, and I promptly return to my seat at the round table. Sharon pats my arm, leans over to me, and kindly whispers, "Nice job!"

Though she's sincere, I feel like the girl who was invited to the party not because the host wanted me there but because someone said it would be the nice thing to do.

Sharon has her eyes fixed on the stage, and I turn to look at her. I notice a large brown leather bracelet on her left arm with the word *BRAVE* tooled into it. I examine her face shadowed by the candle. She's so pretty. She has long, thick brown hair and cool, trendy black glasses. I can tell by the way she holds her body upright and by the settled look in her eyes that, yes, she is brave.

I bet her knees don't shake when she talks.

Dana is back on the stage now, introducing Sharon. This time she holds only one thing: Sharon's book. She clutches it to her chest as she would a treasured Christmas gift and speaks intensely into the microphone while looking out into the audience. She doesn't need a paper to assist her; she's speaking from her heart. Her voice is smooth and calm, her monologue deep with admiration for Sharon and her amazing, life-changing book. She says excitedly, "What a huge gift it is to have Sharon speaking here in our church!"

I wonder if jealousy smells like my sons' hockey bags. You can't even take a breath around them without feeling as though you're going to vomit. I fear that if any of these women walk by me, they'll smell my jealousy. It's oozing from my pores.

This is *my* church, and I feel invisible.

I'm glad Sharon has left the table for the stage. I compare myself to her and the way she's been presented as the finest main course possible. My mind abstracts: *I don't matter.* Once the comparison begins, shame surges, charging through me like an army.

Dana didn't say those nice things about you. She doesn't even know how to pronounce your name! Look at that, Lee. You don't matter. They don't see you. Your family didn't see you, and now your own church can't either. You think you're something and you try hard enough, but it's always the same, isn't it, Lee? Why do you think things will ever be any different?

I try to combat the voice of shame berating me, but it doesn't retreat. I push my shoulders back and lift my head to try to be strong. But it's too late. I've been pierced, right through that tender spot over my heart. I want to run out, to disappear, to get out of this room full of women who want to be inspired.

Why did they even ask you to come?

I look up at Sharon. She's glowing on center stage, already wowing us all, and I smile.

Let me tell you some of the things that come easy to me. It's easy to talk mean to myself, easy to believe everyone is better than me and has it better than me. It's easy to look at another woman and want what she has, and hard to celebrate and be content with what I have. It's easy to post the best pictures of myself on Facebook and quickly delete the rest.

It's easier to yell than to cry, easier to paste a fake smile on my face than to speak my mind. It's easier to grab a glass of wine than to stand awkwardly empty-handed at a party, easier to act as though I have it all together than to admit I'm struggling. Easier to have people over to my house when it's clean than when it looks like something from an episode of *Hoarders*. Easier to speak Christianese to someone who's hurting than to sit in silence and be a witness to her pain.

Not all these things are bad. They're just easier.

It's easier to hide than to be seen. And it's easy to believe everyone else is kinder, more beautiful, and more deserving than I am. It's easier to shrink than to rise.

So in situations like the one I faced at my church, I reached for my smiling mask. When I'm in a room full of women who seem to be better, prettier, and braver than I will ever be, I put on the mask that hides the fact I'm brimming with shame. I've worn it so frequently that it fits my face well. I tie it on tightly and hide behind my friendly Christian facade.

When Sharon's talk ends, the audience erupts with earsplitting applause. Dana returns to the stage and enthusiastically announces that Sharon and I will both be at a table, ready to sign our books. I go to my designated spot and reach into my purse for lipstick. I have to wear lipstick if anyone wants to take a photo with me or I'll look like I'm lipless.

I smack my lips together and lift my head, ready to meet my fans as I peer into a long line of people that bends around the edges of the room.

I keep my mask on and smile.

And I wait.

I feel gusts of air as one by one the women pass by me and walk to Sharon.

All of them. Some nod at me. Others just move on through. I smile awkwardly, trying to be gracious, but it feels as though I'm in seventh grade and have found myself trapped in the wrong classroom after the bell has rung.

When the evening finally ends, I can't get home fast enough. I run into the safety of my dark bedroom and close the door. Alone, I can take the mask off. I fall into my old mahogany rocking chair and let the emotions burst out. I let the ugly cry have its time. I rock back and forth, and sob. Shame and embarrassment fill every part of my body, while my mind and spirit break into little pieces on the floor.

My sweet husband, Chris, quietly walks up the stairs and sits on the bed. He doesn't say anything but waits patiently while I wipe snot off my face.

"I'm quitting," I tell him. "Quitting writing, speaking, and anything that even resembles it. I am done. Finished. How stupid of me to ever think I could do this."

We've been married long enough that Chris knows to let me ramble when I'm in an emotional frame of mind. He knows I don't want fixing. Plus, he's very, very patient, so he just sits and listens.

Finally, when there's space in the air and I'm done with my rant, he quietly says to me, "Lee, is this why you write and speak? To prove you matter? To prove you're good enough?"

I don't answer. The truth sounds so shallow.

"Don't you know that God loves you just as you are?"

No, I don't. But Chris knows my default mode of living is to strive to earn love. I do this with others and with God. I don't *always* write for approval or applause, but sometimes I do. Sometimes I just want to know that the world thinks I am okay. It doesn't seem too much to ask.

It takes me a while to recover from this night. To pick up the broken pieces of me off the floor and then to take a step back and evaluate why I speak and write. After I bandage up my wounded ego, my mind returns to Sharon's bracelet, the one inscribed with

BRAVE. What does it mean to her? Is bravery about standing on a stage and sharing a story, or is it something deeper, something less obvious?

What does it mean to be a brave woman?

I can't get this question out of my head.

When I looked at Sharon that night, I saw her bravery and thought it was beautiful. I couldn't help but think *she* was beautiful. I thought of other times when I was around people who were brave, and I realized I've always experienced awe-inspiring admiration for them. I can always see beauty in the brave one.

So then I wondered, *What is beauty? What is* true *beauty in this world of manufactured messages about flawlessness and youth and the skinny ideal?* Our Western culture constantly bombards us and berates us with messages of how we should be and how short we fall. So we don our masks because we can never measure up. We hide in our dark bedrooms or medicate our anxiety or both. We know we're a hot mess and suspect we always will be. We lose our courage. We become numb.

The more I thought about this, the more I sensed that bravery is at the root of true beauty, the kind that is attractive regardless of one's physical appearance. I began to suspect that the words *brave* and *beautiful* are sisters, maybe even conjoined twins. For the one who chooses to do it, stepping into bravery might be like stepping into a terrible fear. But for those of us watching, we stand in awe, soaking in the magnificent splendor of courage. We know without being told: this is the kind of beauty no magazine can portray and no advertisement can promise to deliver.

So how do we *not* hide from our fear and shame? How do we *not* get sucked into comparing ourselves with one another and measuring our worth by our own ruler? How do we toss the measuring stick aside and act out of bravery every day?

In an effort to find out, I searched for brave women who could answer my questions.

I don't know why I thought they would be hard to find. On the contrary, I couldn't have dodged them if I had tried. But the real surprise was that so many of these women didn't see themselves as either brave or beautiful. This is how powerful our external pressures and inward thoughts can be. Even when we are brave, we deny it. We gloss over the beauty of our own courage by deflecting attention or demurring or … wait for it … comparing. *Well, I don't have it as bad as Jane. I'm not as amazing as Jessica. Lots of women have walked in my shoes. I haven't done anything special.*

I beg to differ. Because along the sidelines of the headline news are inspiring tales of bravery hidden in the mundane details of women's everyday lives—women who make the decision to get up every morning and keep putting one foot in front of the other, doing what is good and right despite the crises and turmoil and dilemmas life tosses at them. These are women steadily making the decision to step out of the boat to walk on the water. Women choosing to take off their masks and live their most authentic life.

In the following pages I will tell you some of their stories and a few more of my own. This book is an exploration of what these sweet sisters, *brave* and *beautiful*, have come to mean to me, what I believe they mean to our Creator, and how they might inspire us to live despite fear and without shame, free of our masks.

I am excited for this adventure and what we might learn from one another.

Won't you join me?

FOR REFLECTION

1. Do you have a protective mask you wear when you feel shame or discomfort? What does your mask say about what's important to you?

2. Think of a time when you felt pain by being compared to others and feeling you were lacking. How did this event shape your beliefs about yourself and/or a choice you made about your future?

3. What makes you shrink back from your hopes, dreams, and relationships?

4. Do you think of yourself as a brave woman? Why or why not?

Two

CONFRONTING

You're imperfect, and you're wired for struggle,
but you are worthy of love and belonging.
Brené Brown, TED Talk

Grandma often told us to not be ugly. She meant in the way we used our words, but even as a child I knew *ugly* was not simply about how we spoke or treated others but how we presented ourselves to the world. Until the day she died, her hair was perfectly curled, her nails professionally manicured, and her pants crisply ironed.

Never mind that she presented this image of beauty and southern charm to the world while she peppered her daughter and grandchildren with alcohol-slurred words that cut so deep they continue to wake me up at night. Her ugly words bruised and destroyed. By covering herself up with pretty clothes and flashy jewelry, Grandma never gave the world a real window to the darkness in her soul.

The high value placed on outward beauty has always baffled me, though it didn't stop me from buying into it. It's just too hard to resist the in-your-face definitions of what beauty is: skinny jeans, skinny lattes, and skinny fashion models who represent only 2 percent of the body types we see.[1] Role models tell us food that makes us skinny is good; food that makes us fat is bad. Whatever you do, don't be fat. Don't be ugly. Because this is one piece of your identity you can control. So you better control it.

I almost died from trying to attain this standard of outward beauty. It hung like an apple on a tree branch I could never reach. Despite developing an eating disorder and exercise addiction, I could never be thin enough, good enough, or pretty enough. In fact, I believed the only thing I'd ever be was a failure, so in 1995 I tried to take my own life. This is the story I tell in *Table in the Darkness*.

With help I stepped off that treadmill of death and chose a different kind of life. But these seductive ideals still tap me on the shoulder and whisper in my ear, calling me back to cultural ideals of beauty. I hate when this happens, when I give the thoughts even the slightest acknowledgment. It twists at my gut and cages up my heart.

Until I see the faces. The faces of those who have gone before me. And I remember the ones who were destroyed by their insatiable hunger to be considered physically beautiful, those who didn't get the second chance I did.

When I'm in venues packed with people, I see them. I glimpse their faces between the spaces of the living. I spot one over the shoulder of a woman at the mall or behind a tree in the busy park, the ones who were pulled so deep into the darkness they lost their lives.

I spend a great number of my working hours at the foot of Jenny's hospital bed. I work at the eating disorders treatment center where she's been admitted. I sit in a brown rocking chair, my hands resting on the mattress, watching her lungs rise and fall. I often volunteer to take the overnight shift as a one-on-one so I can sit with her through the dark hours and pray. My pleas are simple whispers that she can find the strength to feed on something else, something other than the empty bowl of cosmetic beauty.

I sit in the dark and think about Edmund in C. S. Lewis's *The Lion, the Witch and the Wardrobe.* I recall his love for Turkish Delight and how the White Witch conjured an enchanted version of the treat to tempt him into her service. "For she knew," Lewis wrote, "though Edmund did not, that this was enchanted Turkish Delight and that anyone who had once tasted it would want more and more of it, and would even, if they were allowed, go on eating it till they killed themselves."[2] This sweetness would never be enough for him, but Edmund was consumed by his desire and distracted from the villain's true intentions.

I pray for Jenny to find a different food that satisfies. To find hope in a God who loves her.

My friend Shannon, who plays the flute, is sucked into the beauty vortex while in high school. After undertaking an innocent diet, she can fit into her Winterfest dress and receives compliments and approval, so she's hooked. She is the pretty flute-playing thin girl. That's who she is. That's who she will stay.

Or will she?

One summer day before her freshman year of college, Shannon is on the back porch at her friend Maureen's house. They sit on two Adirondack chairs just outside the sliding glass door. Summer air warms their tanned arms. Mac, Maureen's large black dog, sits silently beside them.

Without warning, Mac jumps up, latches on to Shannon's mouth with his sharp teeth, and bites her face.

Maureen screams. Blood pools on the deck. Shannon runs to the bathroom to see what happened. She stands there looking at her bloody face, unsure what to do.

Everything rushes past like a movie on fast-forward, and she finds herself at a nearby medical clinic. Maureen's mother is carrying a plastic bag with pieces of Shannon's lips in it. The doctor says the injury is beyond his level of expertise. She needs a plastic surgeon. Her parents are afraid. They cry, then arrange for a surgeon to meet them at the hospital.

On the way Shannon's arm grows tired from holding the bloody towel to her face. At a stoplight she lowers it to let her arm rest. She looks out the window just as a woman in the car next to her does the same. Shannon sees the woman's mouth open in a scream. Shannon quickly covers her face and thinks, *This can't be good. This can't be good.*

At the hospital the young surgeon, fresh out of medical school, reassures her worried parents. "Don't worry," he says. "I know a lot of tricks."

He puts needles in Shannon's mouth, and suddenly the pain is excruciating. He begins to numb every part of the injury. Shannon wonders about her lips in the bag. *He can't use them*, she thinks logically. The team repairs her mangled face one stitch at a time.

The next morning when she wakes up, she realizes she hasn't eaten anything since before the accident. She wonders how much weight she's lost. Her mouth is stitched up, and she knows it will be hard to eat. She's excited about this new "diet."

But when Shannon looks at her disfigured face in the mirror, she's finally aware of what has happened to her. *You look really bad. This is a bad thing.* Her face is puffy and black and blue, and she has black stitches all over her mouth. There are a few cuts on her cheeks as well. The image is horrifying. She is the pretty flute-playing thin girl who is neither pretty nor talented anymore.

All she has left is being thin, and she holds on to this scrap of her identity with everything she has.

Until her parents force her to get help. The first time in treatment, she does what she's told, but none of it sinks in. But in the near future, when she seeks help on her own, there's a shift.

Because this time Shannon is not being forced. This time she confronts her problem, and this time she gets in the game and fights for her life.

She looks at her body in the mirror and is aware she's severely underweight. In one transformative moment she realizes she's more scared than proud. With this fear comes shame and embarrassment. She's told she should have known better because she's a psychology student doing research on eating disorders. She agrees. She begins to gain some insight into her own mind and heart and feels motivated to change.

Year after year after year, she gets healthier and healthier and healthier.

"I feel like I had the longest, slowest recovery because it never got so bad that I was forced into a quick recovery," she says today. "I had to endure—or had the luxury of, depending on your perspective—the time I needed to figure out who I was, am, and want to be."

Shannon learns to see how her eating disorder was a way of coping with her anxiety and sensitivity. She recognizes a connection between the hurts she experienced in young adulthood and her desire to be liked and to fit in. With the help of therapists, healthy friendships, and her own resolve, she works through her identity issues and realizes she was always more than just the pretty flute-playing thin girl. Slowly Shannon returns to a healthy weight.

In time she gives up the idea of dieting and controlling her body and instead starts to take care of and nurture herself.

She dives into things she's genuinely interested in, and this helps her understand herself better and builds her confidence. She's surrounded by strong women who have their own issues, including those related to body image, but are also intelligent, confident, loving, and kind toward her. She also spends more time outdoors.

Shannon's faith becomes her own. Though baptized as a Catholic, she begins attending a progressive church because she likes the music. She often returns because she wants to sing and connect with others. She goes alone and doesn't feel pressure to explain why she looks the way she does. She doesn't have to discuss whether she exercised or ate before she came or what she plans to eat for the rest of the day. Going to church during her recovery is simultaneously comforting and isolating, but it helps her through.

Recovery gives Shannon the ability to believe she is pretty again. She learns to love her face, because today she has a new definition of beauty. "I base it more on how I feel emotionally about myself, others, and the world. I now see myself as more beautiful when I wake up in the morning and am snuggling with my family than when I was crowned Winterfest queen in high school.

"I am more beautiful now when I am crying and hugging a good friend than when I wore a new outfit and my hair was styled just right. I am more beautiful now as I attempt to play my old flute at my daughter's request than when I was first chair in my high school band. I am more beautiful now in my T-shirt and yoga pants than when I was darkly tanned in a black bikini, receiving compliments about my appearance. I am more beautiful now because I am authentically me."

Jenny wasn't so lucky. Her eating disorder took her life. My heart broke when she died, as it does every time a person is taken by an eating disorder. Anorexia isn't the only killer. There are many more clinically recognized eating disorders. Every one of them is like a drug meant to numb the pain of life. A drug that keeps its victims from being authentically themselves.

Jenny was after beauty. That was her sole desire—to be considered beautiful. And she was. She was a beautiful person when she was fit and healthy and when she was skinny and dying. But she couldn't see it. What she saw was a world that was dark and abusive. So she put her hope in designer clothes and appearances. If she could fix what she looked like—if she could be perfect, exactly like the world thought she should be—then everything would be okay.

She told me this over and over as she went online and purchased thousands of dollars' worth of designer clothes, shoes, and bags. Her longing to transform who she was by weight and clothing was her Turkish Delight. Nothing she bought ever satisfied, and the numbers on the scale were never low enough. She wanted more and more, even as she became more and more sick. How I wish she'd known that true beauty is so much more than the sugary sweetness of the craving that never satisfies. How I wish she'd been able to trust the promise of Jesus, who told his disciples, "I am the bread of life. Whoever comes to me will never be hungry again. Whoever believes in me will never be thirsty" (John 6:35).

On an escalator in the mall I think I see her—those clear eyes, that tender soul. I turn to see if it's her, but she's gone again.

God makes beautiful things out of dust. He trades our ashes for beauty. Shannon is learning the truth of this and confronting the cultural myths daily in her work with those battling their own eating disorders. And while Jenny is no longer here to see the beauty God had for her life, it's my hope that she rests in the arms of her Creator, who says to her, "My sweet girl, I love you just as you are."

I would like to challenge this cultural idea that beauty is defined by a fit body or gap-spaced thighs. I would like to put an end to the obsession with fat and the yearning for thinness. I'm not saying we shouldn't take care of the bodies God gave us. But I am saying we need to change the question from "Do I look fat?" to "Am I being authentically me? Am I being true to who God made me to be?"

Because I see beauty when I see a woman bravely being herself. When she makes the choice to get out of bed when depression or an illness tries to keep her under the covers. When she calls the therapist to ask for help. Or when she stands in front of a crowd and says, "I am an alcoholic." Beauty is the woman who sees her brokenness and acknowledges the scars of life but doesn't try to cover them up or hide behind them. As Brené Brown wrote, "We cultivate love when we allow our most vulnerable and powerful selves to be deeply seen and known, and when we honor the spiritual connection that grows from that offering with trust, respect, kindness, and affection."[3]

Whenever I see the scar on Shannon's face, I see bravery. I see such beauty in what she has overcome and in what she now presents to the world. For us to know one another, we also need to know and touch and love one another's scars and declare them beautiful.

Broken and brave. That's the new definition of beauty you won't find in any magazine or on any runway, but one I can't live without. Can you?

FOR REFLECTION

1. How do you define *beauty*? Can authentic living and cultural ideals of beauty overlap? What are some of the challenges a woman might confront when trying to be both authentically herself and physically beautiful?

2. What "scars" do your friends have that are especially beautiful to you? What are the scars of your life that you try to hide from others? How is learning to love your scars an act of bravery?

3. What factors make it most difficult for you to think about beauty as a character trait rather than a physical trait?

4. Do you believe you are beautiful? If not, what would it take to convince you of your inherent beauty? Name three character traits you possess that you wouldn't hesitate to call beautiful in someone else.

Three

SHIFTING

God never promises to remove us from our struggles. He does
promise, however, to change the way we look at them.
Max Lucado, *Just Like Jesus Devotional*

We sit in silence, I in the chair worn down by so many sitting before me, the therapist opposite, so calm and relaxed with her legs crossed. She holds a yellow notepad in her lap, and her brown eyes stare into me. I've come reluctantly.

"You aren't vulnerable," she says.

I take my watch on and off, the only sound the click of the clasp. I look down at her shoes, these adorable black houndstooth heels, and I want to tell her how much I like her shoes. I want to talk about something else. But this is not why I'm here, in this office, with her analyzing me.

For years I've been seeing a woman who does body-centered healing work to help people deal with emotional trauma. After seeing how my job at the eating disorder treatment center was taking a toll on me, she encouraged me to come here for a different kind of therapy. "You need time and space to process," she said. "You need self-care. Your body is a tangled mess of stress."

Self-care? Self-care seems selfish to me. I need to help other people. This is my calling. Yet I admit something inside me has recently shifted. I have trouble sleeping at night and remembering things. I have painful migraines and an aching stomach.

I can pinpoint the exact day I started to break.

Shelley stumbles over her own feet as she makes her way to the group room. I see the alcohol in her unsteady walk and dilated eyes. I learned the signs as a child because alcoholism was rampant in my family, and I can spot them immediately in the patients I work with. What I don't see right away is that this time Shelley is beyond inebriated.

Before she takes her seat with the group, I ask her to step out of the room. Her eyes cloud with dark anger. She knows I know. I'll ruin her high, I'll be her buzzkill, and she doesn't like it. She begins to yell expletives at me as we walk into the hallway.

Somehow I convince her to go upstairs to a small exam room. I awkwardly help her sit on the table covered with wax paper. Her stream of consciousness spills out of her mouth, and most of her words are harsh spurts of anger toward me for making her sit in this room. I stand close to her, waiting for the doctor I've paged to come and assess her. The odor of alcohol is so pungent it makes me nauseated.

My heart breaks once again.

After almost nine years working in this treatment center, I think I've grown accustomed to situations such as this, and yet I haven't. Each time I watch a patient who struggles with both an eating disorder and substance abuse begin to crack, I crack with her. Some patients more than others break me wide open. Shelley is one of those. I spent hours with her, listening to her stories of trauma and abuse at the hands of psychiatric facilities when she was younger, and I ached when I learned of her current tumultuous life on the street. She has no real place to call home. And now as I stay with her, I hope for her, that she will see what I see: that the wounded girl and intelligent woman with a sassy personality and warm heart has a future. I want to fix her pain.

I can't seem to realize it isn't my job to fix her.

Shelley continues to cuss me out as she wobbles on the table.

The scene unfolds exactly opposite of how I want it to, and before we know it, there are three police officers standing in the doorway. Behind them, a large man with too much hair on his face stands ready with a stretcher. I know of her terror of being strapped down, so I say to the men, "Please, can we try to get her to walk out with you? Does she have to be strapped down?"

One of the officers unapologetically says, "Only if she doesn't comply."

Shelley's curses turn to yelling, and the officers have no time for her games. They've seen this before, an inebriated girl physically resisting the fact they must get her to a detox facility. Routine for them. But I want to convince them to stop. To tell them, "You can't see her in there and you don't know her!" My heart drops to the floor as they strap her screaming and flailing body to the stretcher. There are too many people around her, and she can't find air. I stand behind the men who block me, and I find a tiny space between them. I see her hair falling messily on her face and drool coming out of her mouth.

"Hold on!" I say. I push through the bodies and get close to her. "Hey, Shelley ... it is going to be okay. You are going to be okay." I wipe her drool off her face with my sleeve and tenderly push her hair behind her ear. Her eyes stare back at me with wild fear.

They wheel her away. Her screams penetrate the empty hall and pierce me. I shake uncontrollably as I stare into nothing. The incident sends me spinning for days. My nights are marked by relentless insomnia, my mornings by panic-stricken worry. It hasn't always been this way.

Later that week is when the woman helping me heal notices my own weariness and recommends therapy. I dig my heels in like a stubborn mule, but my body insists I need to follow her advice. So I agree, begrudgingly, to make an appointment.

I don't want to be the broken one who needs fixing again. I don't want to be sitting in this chair across from the professional with the stunning shoes. I don't want to be in this room.

I hear the whispers of the past telling me to "just let go and let God." And then I feel the hot shame rushing through my veins.

She wastes no time. "You aren't vulnerable."

I want to throw something at her. I want to kick her in the knee. She doesn't see any of this anger because I don't show her.

"Not vulnerable?" I crisply respond. "Ask my friends. They will say I am vulnerable."

She doesn't say anything, just scribbles on her yellow notepad.

"I just wrote a book detailing all my darkest and grossest moments and shared it with the world. How is that *not* vulnerable?" I say.

My face heats up and my thoughts begin to spin.

No answer.

I feel like I'm back in the principal's office, pleading my case that I didn't throw red chalk into Brandy Moore's long blonde hair, even though I actually did.

The therapist tilts her head and continues to look through me.

I explain, "I am the girl standing on the stage, talking about how wonderful my life is and how beautiful it is without an eating disorder, without depression. And it is! I'm speaking the truth!"

After many long, long seconds she quietly says, "Ah yes. I am not saying you aren't speaking the truth, Lee. But what is it about those situations that is different from this situation in this room, with me, right now?"

I have this place in my abdomen where my muscle is split from childbirth. It never repaired itself. Sometimes when I sit up, it pokes out and I have to wiggle it back into place. Right now I feel like I'm that piece of muscle poking out where it isn't supposed to be, and I know the therapist doesn't want me to put it back into place. She wants me to sit in the awkwardness of it.

This is the shift: Someone has pointed out this displaced muscle and forced me to look at it with new eyes. Something is telling me I need to make a closer examination so I can continue my healing. After twenty years of recovery, it's time to shift positions for my own good. I know somewhere deep inside me that this woman is willing to help me do the work.

I didn't think therapy would be this hard. After all, I'd been to therapy before. Years of therapy. Plus, I work at a treatment center with therapists every day, coleading therapy groups. I challenge patients daily not to hide their secret places of pain and shame but to bring them out into the open where they can be tended. I work tirelessly to create safe places for them to be real, honest, and vulnerable so they can heal. So they can be whole. I don't have to be vulnerable in my work, which is about the patients, not me. They're on their own journey. I'm only walking alongside and helping them feel safe.

To me, this job is my ultimate sweet spot, my reason for being alive. I get to help others become the amazing and beautiful people God created them to be.

I can tell patients what to do, but am I doing it in my own life? I was—until I wasn't. The eating isn't a struggle for me anymore, but the weight of this job is beginning to feel like a heavy dumbbell on my back. I thought I was being brave by bucking up and surviving the struggle. Yet so much is happening inside me, and I don't want to talk about it.

Because here's the thing: I don't ever ask for help. I'll tell *you* to ask for help, and I'll be there for you in a heartbeat if you need anything. But helping me? No, thank you. I'll do it on my own. I am independent, self-sufficient, and motivated.

This happens in my faith too. *It's okay, God. I can push through. Don't worry about me.* My stubbornness even keeps me from needing God! How many times will I have to relearn these lessons?

After a moment of reflection I see the therapist is right. And it costs me. Not being vulnerable and not asking for help cost all of us. My body is exhausted, my heart saddened by so much grief, and my hope tainted. Only by first being vulnerable in this therapist's office will I hopefully gain what I need so I can be more vulnerable in my own everyday life.

"I *am* vulnerable!" I repeat. Now I'm mad.

Her mouth turns up in a slight smile.

"You are vulnerable when you can be in charge of the situation. When you can control it in a book or on a stage. I want you to be vulnerable here, without controlling or editing yourself. That is the only way I can work with you."

I don't respond. She puts her words right into that spot in my chest where I hold myself together. The spot I white-knuckle on a daily basis. I can't deny that I am a bona fide control freak. Early on as a little girl, I realized that if I didn't live this way, life would come back to haunt me.

Here in this office, staring at this woman, I find myself face to face with what I fear most. This is what bravery must look like for me: admitting some of my own anger at my mother, unpacking my insatiable need for control, and admitting that, *yes*, despite being a Christian, I sometimes still feel the dark hand of depression hooking its bony finger into my heart and trying to drag me back into the pit.

My denial isn't working anymore. Having control, managing life with my mask and my tight grip, and letting the world see my real self only when I'm in charge or when I choose—these are old and tired ways of coping.

"Okay," I finally say. "Where do we start?"

This is my brave. You see, it scares me for you to really know me. What if you don't like these icky parts of me? What if I actually need someone or must be called *needy*? The thought is unbearable. So I do life on my own. I cry only in spaces where I am alone or with only my husband. I buck up and act pretty and kind and polite. Because that's what we do, right? We hold it all together all by ourselves for our families and everyone around us because we don't want to be a burden to anyone. Not even to God.

We want to be Wonder Woman, who does it all so sweetly and then says, "Oh, what a blessing."

Can we just cut the nonsense? Life isn't that simple. Life isn't that easy. We aren't perfect. We are broken. If we weren't, why would we need a Savior?

I want to do life differently. I want to shift the way I cope so I can be healthier. I want this uncomfortable poking in my gut to help me allow others to show me how to be brave. You can ask me to jump out of a plane, speak in front of thousands of people, or even walk into a women's conference dressed in a banana suit (which I have done). All these things are fun and I don't hesitate to do them. But this—getting really raw in an unedited and vulnerable way in therapy—scares the pants right off me. Even so, I agree wtih Henri Nouwen, who wrote,

> The main question is "Do you own your pain?" As long as you do not own your pain—that is, integrate your pain into your way of being in the world—the danger exists that you will use the other to seek healing for yourself. When you speak to others about your pain without fully owning it, you expect something from them that they cannot give. As a result, you will feel frustrated, and those you wanted to help will feel confused, disappointed, or even further burdened.[1]

I don't know about you, friends, but I don't want to go through my life unconscious, running from my pain. I did that once, and it didn't work. I don't want to spend my days anxious, panicking because my spirit knows what my mind struggles to admit: I can't do this alone.

"Make friends with your needs," psychologists Henry Cloud and John Townsend wrote in their book *Safe People*. "Welcome them. They are a gift from God, designed to draw you into relationship with him and with his safe people. Your needs are the cure to the sin of self-sufficiency."[2]

Now more than ever I want to open that door to those messy, awkward, and often ugly places of my life and invite the willing to pull up a chair and look around. Why? Because this is how we truly help one another and grow together—*together*. This is how we give up our self-important control so that God can take over and do his work in us and through us.

Together, let's do this!

FOR REFLECTION

1. Do you feel anything shifting in your own life? What changes are you sensing? What are the signs? What do you need to agree to in order to move forward?

2. Do you find it easy or difficult to be vulnerable? What makes you reluctant to reveal your authentic self to others? What makes this easier for you?

3. What do you try to be for others that, deep inside, you believe you are not (for example, vulnerable, confident, peaceful, hopeful)? What do you need to do to become the person you really want to be? How might your present relationships with others make this easier or more difficult?

4. What do you hope to learn from this book?

Four

TELLING

There is no greater agony than bearing an untold story inside you.

Maya Angelou, *Rainbow in the Cloud*

At five years old, spunky Amy is constantly flipping and tumbling all over the house. Gymnastics training seems like the perfect way to direct her bubbling energy. And the gym, run by Peter Johnson and his mother, is the premier gymnastics place in town. With a hefty price tag and rigorous practice regimen, it's the place to be.

Around age seven, Amy begins to shine as a gymnast. Coach Peter constantly gushes to anyone who will listen about Amy's talent and extraordinary poise during competitions.

Amy devotes her young life to gymnastics until she's twelve. After a meet with yet another first-place win, she announces to her mom, "I want to quit."

The decision seems to come out of nowhere. Her mom, Keri, discusses it with Amy over many days, uncertain what provoked the sudden choice to abandon an activity she loves. In the end Keri decides to honor her daughter's wishes; she doesn't want to push her.

One evening while Amy is still in middle school, she comes downstairs for dinner and sees her mom standing at the kitchen counter, staring off into the living room. Her mom turns to her with serious eyes. "Did you see who was on the news tonight?"

"No."

"It was your old gymnastics coach!"

Amy grabs a glass from the cabinet. "Oh? Why?"

"He's being charged with inappropriately touching young girls."

Amy doesn't respond. Her dad and siblings are away at a basketball game. She pours herself something to drink, sits down with her mother, then picks up her fork and begins to eat.

Keri's eyes squint with worry. "Amy, did he ever inappropriately touch you?"

Amy's mind returns to that embarrassing day at the gym. She was seven the first time Peter took her behind the big blue mats to do special stretches. It felt funny and wrong, but she wasn't sure. Other girls sometimes went with him behind the mats too, so Amy told herself it was probably okay.

But when it kept happening, Amy eventually decided she needed to ask. One day during the vault rotation, Amy tapped her friend Molly on the shoulder. She was scared to ask this strange question but found the courage.

"Hey, does Peter ever touch you weird behind the mat?" Amy whispered.

Molly curled her lip and looked at Amy as if she'd said something incredibly stupid. "Um, no!"

Amy was embarrassed. Molly's response and disgusted expression were seared in Amy's mind.

Over dinner in the kitchen, Amy says to her mom, "No. Not that I can think of."

"Okay, tell me something," Keri says. "Was there ever a time when you were like, *Hmmm, this is really weird*?"

Amy looks up at the ceiling, takes a sip of her milk, then says, "Sometimes he would take girls behind the mat for special stretching. That was kind of weird."

"Did he ever do that to you?"

"No."

The conversation stops there and Keri believes her daughter. She has no reason not to.

Six girls come forward at once to accuse Peter, and Amy witnesses the way they're treated by parents, other kids, and the public. Some call the girls liars and believe they're making up stories, trying to get money. She watches the scenes unfold at school and on the news. She doesn't want to get involved, and she really doesn't want to embarrass her family. She doesn't want anyone to hate them. Plus, she still isn't sure whether what Peter did to her was actually wrong.

She stays quiet.

Holding the secret is really hard. She buries it deep inside and tries not to think about it. But the case moves forward and gets so much media attention that the secret follows her everywhere. She wants so badly to tell her friends from the gym. She wants to ask if it happened to them too. But every time the words begin to come out of her mouth, she remembers Molly's appalled look and holds her tongue.

Her mom is asked to write a letter supporting Peter and the gym, and Amy encourages her to do so. She even signs a statement of her own saying he didn't touch her inappropriately.

One day at lunchtime in the large middle school cafeteria, Amy sits with her friends at their usual spot, a table close to the bright windows. A girl named Maddy joins them. Maddy usually sits at a different table.

The case against Peter comes up. Amy's secret scratches at her like a wool sweater. The warm sun beats through the window onto her back, and she begins to sweat. The girls at the table keep talking about the case, and before Amy has time to think, the words come out of her mouth very quietly.

"He molested me."

Two of the girls look at Amy, and one of them says, "He molested me too." All three of them begin to cry. Then they get up to go talk privately in the bathroom. An unspoken bond forms among them, anchored in the relief of not carrying their secrets alone.

Maddy, who has overheard the entire conversation, goes home and tells her mom. Maddy's mom calls Keri.

Later that evening Amy's mom comes into Amy's bedroom, a room decorated in tie-dyed wallpaper and bright, fluffy pillows. Amy has recently kept it dark, the shades drawn and the pillows tossed on the floor. A vault of her secret. Her mom sits down on her bed and asks what happened in the lunchroom. Amy knows she knows. But Amy is scared to tell. Embarrassed.

She looks at her mom, the fear and worry in her eyes, and she knows this is her time to finally come clean. She may not get another chance to speak the truth. Amy suddenly realizes she needs to tell, because anything is better than holding the secret on her own.

"Mom, when I was a little girl, Peter molested me." She cries and shakes as she says this. It's like all the air that had been trapped inside comes out. Despite the embarrassment of it, she's finally unburdened. And she cries deep, heavy sobs of relief.

Telling the truth is only the first challenge. With the help and protection of her parents, Amy soon has to tell her story to police officers, lawyers, and even social workers. Over and over again, she's asked about every detail.

Amy continues to attend school and participates in her new sport on the cheer team, but she walks through the halls afraid. She has crossed the divide, and there are plenty of people who don't like the families who are accusing a beloved coach of something so heinous. Who will whisper behind her back and call her a liar? Who will run home and talk about her to their parents? Who is on her side? Who is not? She isn't always sure, and this makes daily life terrifying.

After being absent one day, Amy takes her mother's note to her assigned secretary, per school procedure. The woman used to work at Peter's gym. She takes Amy's note and scribbles something on the paper, then throws it back at her. Her eyes burn into Amy.

Keri calls the office to have Amy assigned to a different secretary.

The first traumatizing detailing of Amy's story happens at child protective services.

The place is small and smells musty. There is a small table to the left and children's toys spread throughout the waiting area. The walls are gray; the tables and the carpet are old, dusty, and gray. Everything is gray.

She wonders if her parents will have to hear this, if they will have to listen to all the ways Peter touched her. She's relieved when the child protective services agents ask her parents to stay in the waiting room. Amy is ushered into a tiny room with a camera in the top right corner looking down on her. The two adults, both middle aged with brown hair, are kind in their questioning but make sure to get into the nitty-gritty details they need to report. They dig deep.

Amy is wearing a skirt and deeply regrets this choice of clothing. The agents want her to demonstrate what happened to her. She isn't expecting this. Luckily, one of them has a pair of sweatpants in her car and lends them to Amy.

Amy sits on the floor with her bottom against the couch and her legs spread wide, explaining, showing. It's traumatizing. Their questions sicken her. The details and her statements will be given to the defense team so they can interrogate her when she testifies. The session lasts more than an hour and a half and is seared into her memory forever.

On the stand in the courtroom, the bravery inside this young woman shines. Amy's parents were subpoenaed by Peter's lawyer and therefore not allowed in the courtroom. Amy is relieved and embarrassed. Giving her statement to child protective services was difficult enough. Repeating it to a room of people is equally hard. While she knows her mom wanted to be there to support her, Amy is glad her mom won't hear it all.

The defense lawyer, a short, round, balding man who looks like John Belushi, goes after her with belligerent questioning. He holds up the document Amy signed and the letter her mom wrote.

"Did you or did you not sign this document?"

"Yes," Amy says.

He leans forward, his head barely higher than the witness stand. "Do you *always* sign things without reading them?"

Amy's lawyer intervenes. "Objection. Let's please remind the court and the jury the witness is thirteen years old."

Her lawyer looks at her with eyes of empathy. She believes he means to bring Peter to justice. This case is more than a few days' work for him.

While she's on the stand testifying against Peter, they play portions of the video taken by child protective services. The pressure is too much for her, and she trembles and begins to cry. She tries to pull herself together but is overwhelmed.

The judge says, "We need to take a recess."

"No. I'm fine," Amy says. But the judge dismisses the court for ten minutes.

She composes herself and returns to the courtroom, where she's interrogated for four hours. Back and forth the attorneys fight and argue and question. The defense attorney works to poke holes in her story while her lawyer does everything possible to help her stay calm. The eyes of Peter's mother scare her the most. Though Amy's family members aren't allowed in court, somehow Peter's family is. They stare Amy down, but she refuses to be crushed. At thirteen she understands right and wrong and knows now that everything Peter did to her was wrong.

While on the stand, Amy looks Peter in the eye because she wants him to know how much his actions affected her. It's her time to tell her story. The more she says and the more she affirms the truth with her words, the stronger she becomes.

In the end, Peter Johnson is found guilty on seven of the fifteen charges of sex crimes brought against him. Amy's is one of them.

Telling our stories is only the beginning of the healing process, but as the first step, it's often the hardest.

Now Amy is a thriving adult who can express gratitude for Maddy's decision to tell what she overheard that day in the cafeteria. Amy believes that if Keri hadn't found out the truth from Maddy's mom, Amy might have kept her painful secret indefinitely.

It's in the telling of our stories that we begin to heal. Our stories need to be told. Our truth needs to be heard. When we speak the truth and bring it into the light, the darkness of our pain starts to lose its grip. Ironically, when we keep our stories locked away in a cage hidden from the world, they gain power over us. They gain strength in our bodies and our minds.

In my line of work I have seen this happen hundreds of times. Those who dare to expose their pain to a safe person or group of people find freedom. They can disconnect that U-Haul of shame from their lives and take steps to move on. Those who don't tell get worse, sick from the inside out as their pain festers and grows in their bodies.

"Traumatized people chronically feel unsafe inside their bodies," said psychiatrist Bessel van der Kolk in *The Body Keeps the Score: Brain, Mind, and Body in the Healing of Trauma*. "The past is alive in the form of gnawing interior discomfort. Their bodies are constantly bombarded by visceral warning signs, and, in an attempt to control these processes, they often become expert at ignoring their gut feelings and in numbing awareness of what is played out inside. They learn to hide from their selves."[1]

Of course, healing doesn't happen right away.

When the trial against Peter ended, Amy tried to resume her life, but the emotional trauma inflicted on her was painful and deep. Her former gymnastics teammates, some of whom lost their cases against Peter because of insufficient evidence, never talked about that season of their lives. They all just tried to repair what had been torn apart by this one man. Amy fell into step with a wild crowd and made choices that frustrated, worried, and angered her parents.

It was a dark time.

Her parents—grappling with their own pain over not being able to protect their daughter from a nightmare—made an important choice. Instead of growing bitter and angry, instead of wallowing in blame, they brought their family together and made a commitment to work through the pain and heal. They enlisted the help of qualified, skilled therapists and an intimate community of friends to help them navigate the muddy waters of this horrible situation. They set their minds and hearts on moving toward hope. "Being able to feel safe with other people is probably the single most important aspect of mental health," van der Kolk said. "Safe connections are fundamental to meaningful and satisfying lives."[2]

In time Amy's trauma lessened. The negative effects faded. She began to feel safe in her own body again. While the crisis was not what Amy would have wished for her childhood or for her family, she has emerged braver and stronger.

"Telling my story did help me," she tells me with a confident spark in her voice. "I am so open about this. I am not reserved or keeping it from anyone. This story has shaped me as a person. I think it's important for people to know that it's okay to come forward and that everyone goes through tough things. And yes, this did bring out some independence and strength in me when I was sitting up there on that stand. A strength I didn't even know I had.

"At this point in my life, I see the situation as a blessing and not a curse. It has helped me to make my faith my own. There are so many lessons to be learned in a traumatic situation like this. My faith is so much stronger now, and because it is stronger, I have been able to come to terms with everything. Someday I would love to be a child advocate to help other little girls speak up and not be afraid."

I'm not sure I've met a young woman who's braver than Amy. Her courage and openness help me believe that despite how horrible things can be, we can overcome. And not only overcome but turn the tables on our hurts, as Amy hopes to do as a child advocate.

We need to tell our stories, but we also need to exercise discernment in who we tell them to. Not everyone can hold our stories with tenderness and care. We need to develop trusting relationships before we allow someone to hold our stories. Sometimes we can begin with a professional therapist, who can help us identify others who are safe. Because Amy was initially able to tell her story in a safe place, today it's easier for her to talk about the experience publicly.

This is how I've also found comfort in the sharing of my most vulnerable self. Since beginning a new journey with my therapist and sharing the details of my story with people who love God and me, God has continued his healing work in me from the inside out. The stories burning a hole inside you are the stories you need to get out of your body, where they can no longer hold any power over you.

FOR REFLECTION

1. Have you kept secret any stories you're ashamed of? How do you think your secret has affected you physically? Emotionally? Spiritually?

2. What prevents you from telling your story? Amy feared bringing embarrassment and criticism to her family. If you were a friend of young Amy, what would you say to her about this fear?

3. Have you ever told your story to someone and been ridiculed, rejected, or judged? How do you think a truly safe person might respond to your story? What would it take for you to find such a person and risk talking to him or her?

4. In what ways can you be a safe person for other women who have painful stories to tell?

Five

HOPING

*Hope deferred makes the heart sick, but a
dream fulfilled is a tree of life.*

Proverbs 13:12

Heather Jo sits in her eighth-grade home economics class, sewing a pillow. The shape is uneven and the stuffing bulky, so she decides to rip open the seams and try again. She knows that if she keeps trying hard enough, it has to work eventually. Stitch by stitch, she painstakingly pulls apart days of work. With the soft cloth in her hand, she returns to a thought that's been floating in her mind for the past few days, ever since her social studies teacher spoke of displaced children from other countries. *Everyone needs a parent.* The sentence plays like a repetitive song in her head. She keeps returning to that sentence, then packs it away for later reflection.

While other girls are thinking of boys and puberty, Heather Jo notices children and parents everywhere. She's drawn to the children in shops and at the grocery store, wondering about those who don't have a parent walking with them down the aisles or a parent telling them to watch out for cars in the parking lot. She thinks about them at night after her mom comes to tell her good night and kisses her on the cheek. She wonders, *Who is kissing those children?*

In college she meets and falls in love with Jason. A contrast to her bubbly and fast-talking personality, Jason is quiet and introspective. She has a clear expectation though. Whomever she marries needs to support her burning desire to be a parent to orphans. The plight of these children has solidified in her mind, and she feels strongly the road to adoption is meant for her. Why else would her heart break at the mere thought of these little ones longing for love?

Jason is on board. One of the songs they hear playing on the night of their engagement is David Wilcox's song "Hold It Up to the Light." After they marry, this becomes a mantra for them on their journey together. Whenever there's a decision to make, Jason reminds Heather Jo to hold it up to the light.

> *If I keep my eyes open and look where I should*
> *Somehow all of the signs are in sight*
> *If I hold it up to the light.*[1]

Anxious for the desires of her heart to come to fruition, Heather Jo waits patiently, repeatedly asking God like a child on Christmas morning, *Now? Now is it time?*

They have two girls of their own before the answer seems to be yes. The haze of parenting two little girls saturates her days, and she lives in the space where her greatest desire is a clean floor and a full night's sleep.

Sitting by her fireplace, she sees an advertisement in the Sunday paper about children waiting in the foster care system. Children who need parents.

Without hesitation she visits the website, searching the faces of these boys and girls of all ages, looking deep into their eyes. Their sweet eyes long for someone to love them. Take care of them. Parent them.

Now, God? Is it time?

She sees a picture of Sydney and Mark. They sit together on a bench, with colorful leaves on the ground from the fall foliage. They're half siblings with the same birth father, ages fourteen and nine, left to be raised by a mother who recently died. They were placed in foster care to await adoption. They have no one. No next of kin wanted them. In the photo, Sydney, the nine-year-old, looks down at the ground, her eyes so sad and heavy looking. Heather Jo sees these two children and is drawn to them.

Yes, yes. The green light begins to shine. Both Jason and Heather Jo begin to open the door to the dream that's lived so long within her.

One night they're lying in bed, talking about their life with their two daughters and how healthy and happy these little girls are. They are thriving in their schools and comfortable in their home and family. Year after year, the Christmas card bears the smiling faces of this cheerful and content family of four.

"Why mess with something that's working?" one of them asks.

The next morning Heather Jo is back in the chair by the fireplace, praying and reading her Bible, hoping for clarity. As she reads she discovers a card tucked between two pages. It's from her Mothers of Preschoolers group, and it bears a quote from Pastor Rick Warren:

> Life is a series of problems: Either you are in one now, you're just coming out of one, or you're getting ready to go into another one. The reason for this is that God is more interested in your character than your comfort.... We can be reasonably happy here on earth, but that's not the goal of life. The goal is to grow in character, in Christ-likeness.[2]

They move forward with fostering them with the hope of adopting them in the future.

Sydney and Mark walk in through the foyer of the warm home to bedrooms they can call their own.

The little girls hug them and invite them in. Sydney and Mark are hesitant and quiet, having been in various homes already, none of them permanent. The littlest girl grabs Sydney's hand and takes her on a tour. Excitedly she shows Sydney her dolls and her toys and the pretty pink room Sydney will now sleep in. Mark stands in the entrance, unsure what to do. Unsure if he belongs. Unsure if he should trust this family.

They settle in and sit down at the round table for dinner while Heather Jo retrieves the milk from the fridge. She watches them from the kitchen and thinks, *The six of us, a family.*

She hears the little ones asking questions and sees the older ones relax a little. Her dream, so long growing in her heart, is finally reality. Right here at her dining room table. "Thank you, Lord," she whispers. "Thank you, Lord."

The normal challenges arise as the family adjusts to Sydney and Mark, but nothing Heather Jo and Jason haven't anticipated. Until it all begins to quickly unravel. Four months into their new life, this dream starts to come apart at the seams.

Heather Jo takes Sydney to a stylist to help with her unruly hair and leaves the girls home alone with Mark for the first time. He's been doing well; Heather Jo feels it's safe. When she returns, her daughter is courageous enough to tell her the awful, true details. Mark made inappropriate choices with one of her daughters while he was alone with them.

"Unsafe. The situation is unsafe," the social workers and counselors say to them. "The boy needs to be removed from the home." Heather Jo and Jason are afraid. Already they love Mark as their own. How can they take him away from his sister? An unanswered question also rises to the surface: Is Sydney even safe around him? They're devastated and worried. Where will he go? Who will take care of him? How will he get help for his unfortunate choices? They don't know.

They only know that to protect the girls, they need to let him go.

Is this really God's plan? Heather Jo asks herself. *Was this not the right time? Did I make a mistake? How did this happen?*

On a rainy day in April, Mark's social worker takes him away from their home. The family hugs him and he shows very little emotion. This young boy's emotional armor is strong. Heather Jo worries that no amount of affection can break through.

As quickly as he arrived, Mark is gone. Heather Jo grieves the loss as she would her own child.

In the midst of heartbreak, Heather Jo and Jason set their focus on healing the family, repairing what has occurred and integrating Sydney into the home. Heather Jo is hopeful Sydney can grow some roots and find some stability. They proceed to legally adopt her, hoping this will help Sydney know how much they want her.

The proceedings have the opposite effect.

The adoption triggers Sydney's reactive attachment disorder. She lashes out in ways that are above and beyond a typical preteen girl. Day after day the screaming and the angry outbursts morph into terrifying rages. The police arrive as backup when Sydney's rage threatens others. Social workers explain to the family that Sydney still has the needs of a baby. She's missed those critical years of attachment and belonging. Heather Jo and Jason start to wonder if they had unfair expectations of this girl. They try to adjust so they can give her what she needs.

They seek counseling and prayer in multiple places, hoping to find help for this emotionally unstable girl. They learn more about Sydney and Mark and find they were both sexually abused in violent ways when they were younger. Heather Jo's heart breaks at this news.

The situation continues to fall apart. Sleepless nights become the norm for Heather Jo and Jason, and fear pervades the air in the home as the years drag on.

"There are five of us in a sinking ship, and we're trying to save one while the rest of us drown," Jason says to Heather Jo. "And we aren't even saving the one—we're all drowning."

Heather Jo's dream has become a nightmare.

She knows they have to find a plan B, but she's confused and perplexed by this. Why would God offer her this vision, this desire of her heart, only to fulfill it and then rip it from her in such a painful manner? Now when they hold the situation up to the light, it's so messy they can't see any answers.

Through counsel with the team that's now helping the family, one truth becomes clear: Sydney needs a home where there are no other children. She needs a place where she can heal from her trauma and potentially have a corrective experience for the earlier part of her life. This will take full-time care and attention from someone who isn't also parenting two little girls reeling from the turmoil inflicted by Mark.

There are no clear-cut answers to this challenging problem. Heather Jo prays and waits, trying to settle the constant storm in her home.

The answer comes in the grace of a phone call. Before Sydney was placed with Heather Jo and Jason, she lived with foster parents, Terry and Joe, who have an older son who will soon be leaving for college, so they can focus exclusively on Sydney. They love Sydney too and have continued to play a role in her life since she left their care.

Terry calls and says, "We will do whatever the family needs. Even if it means taking Sydney back. We're open to that option if it's the right move for Sydney."

How do you let go of a dream that's been growing inside you for most of your life? How do you surrender to the death of this dream—once so alive and colorful and beautiful, now dark and messy and unfathomable? And how do you not feel tricked, as if God wasn't in the decisions in the first place? Why would he ask you to follow a dream and then snatch it out of your hand, leaving wounded people behind?

These are the questions facing Heather Jo, whose dream died not once but twice.

She has no answers. She has only trust. She simply trusts that God is bigger than any of it and will direct her next step. "He will not let you stumble," she reads in her Bible, "the one who watches over you will not slumber" (Ps. 121:3).

They tell Sydney about the option to return to Terry and Joe, fearing her anger and the hurtful words she'll probably throw back at them. Sydney's response is unlike what they expect. She wants to go back to Terry's. Somewhere in her, she knows it is better for her. Sydney was with Terry when she found out her mother had died. Terry is the only one Sydney has ever actually attached to.

Everyone knows this is the right decision. But Sydney's eyes take on the look that had made Heather Jo's heart ache back when she first saw the siblings' picture on the website. They're the eyes of a little girl longing for something she believes she can never have, something she wants more than anything in the world. Every time Heather Jo and Jason previously offered Sydney love, she reacted with violent resistance born of great fear. But this time she's solemn and resolved.

Heather Jo packs Sydney's room while she's at school, removing the pink comforter and stuffed animals they won at the amusement park. She packs away the photos of the family and the trendy clothes Sydney picked out at the mall. Her heart breaks open and resembles the shattered pieces of her dream.

The only way for Heather Jo to move forward is to hold everything loosely, trusting it is all God's, both the messy and the beautiful parts. She finds courage in her faith, the only thing that helps her slowly let go of these children. None of it makes any sense to her. She leans on friends who sit with her in her pain, not offering platitudes but being present with her.

Heather Jo walks around her home in a fog. Her mind spins with questions and she replays decisions over and over. Her tortured mind attacks her. *Was the dream only mine and not God's too? Was all this my fault?* Memories and questions berate her, but no tears come, just an ache deep in her bones.

She walks in and out of rooms with no real reason but just wanders as if she's looking for something or someone. *What if Mark and Sydney were to be here only for a season?* The familiar words from

Ecclesiastes offer truth but not comfort. "For everything there is a season, a time for every activity under heaven.… A time to cry and a time to laugh. A time to grieve and a time to dance" (3:1, 4). She thinks that maybe because they were here, Sydney's and Mark's pasts could come to light. *What if now both of them can get the help they need?* She doesn't know the answers this side of heaven.

Sydney is gone, her bedroom bare and the family table flanked by two empty chairs. That night Heather Jo's friends sense her and Jason's pain and invite them out for dinner. Three other couples have walked along this road with them. No words need to be spoken. They are friends who are just hoping to help hold some of their pain.

They sit at a long table, staring at their menus, all of them sensing Heather Jo isn't simply in grief but in shock. They ask her what she wants to eat. They ask her if she wants to talk about what's happened. She doesn't. She holds her anxiety and sorrow close, so her friends love her in the only way they know how. They tell funny stories to try to brighten the mood. Heather Jo is engaged and laughing while dessert is being passed around the table, until out of nowhere something happens. Her mood changes without warning. She freezes and her eyes glaze over.

Her grief has grown too large for her body. She starts to convulse and suddenly begins to vomit. She isn't aware of what is happening. Two of her girlfriends lean in and try to shelter her from the people in the restaurant now looking at her. They try to help her body settle. The scene is traumatic for everyone watching. They clean up the vomit. They try to console and comfort her, but nothing works.

Jason rushes into action and quickly swoops her up out of the restaurant. His beautiful wife, now in a zombie-like state. Once outside, her lungs fill with air. She flails and screams. Her cries are the guttural moans of a mother who has lost her children. Jason clumsily gets her into the car, where she begins kicking the dashboard, door, and windshield. Her force is so powerful the windshield cracks.

Out of her mind with grief and pain, her body erupts again in a violent rush of vomiting and screaming.

At their home, Jason carries her into the house and into the shower, where she stays, sobbing. Heather Jo cries out to God, her heart broken, her dream so quickly gone like the water down the drain, slipping away.

Heather Jo's grieving, just like her dream, took time.

When she was able to, she processed the grief and disappointment and confusion in therapy. She came to understand why the children weren't ready for a forever home. She could see from this vantage that her original family of four reeled from the trauma Mark caused. It made sense that Sydney couldn't attach to them. And today Heather Jo knows beyond a doubt that her marriage would never have survived had Sydney stayed in their home. She knows that releasing her dream was right, even though it was a sacrifice she never expected to make.

Even now she continues to question, ponder, and grieve. But nothing can erase the pain.

"I just keep saying, this world is messed up," Heather Jo tells me. "I longed for adoption to be part of my story, and with all that happened, it broke my heart. But I trust there is a much bigger story than my own being told in all of this, that good will come out of it. That's what gives me hope."

Hope. Heather Jo's trust in God in the face of pain is her bravery. Because she trusts, she also can hope, and hope is her supreme beauty.

This kind of faith astonishes me. Her heart senses what her mind can't yet grasp: "It is in and through the travail of the pains of suffering that God creates something new," philosopher James Olthuis wrote in *The Beautiful Risk.* "God weeps for us. God mourns with those who mourn—and 'where God is at work, mourning is not the end.' Then comes the promise of something new, the dawn of a morning of hope, the promise that God will turn mourning into joy and replace sorrow with gladness."[3]

None of this—stepping out in faith, following our dreams, or even letting dreams die—is without pain. That's why it's so difficult. It takes courage to take the beautiful risk of following a dream without a guaranteed outcome; it takes even more boldness to follow the dream without knowing whether you can accept the outcome. True bravery recognizes the need to release our vision and even our desire to control as much as possible, so our dreams can be fulfilled as God sees fit. It takes real trust to believe God is the author of our dreams even if they don't play out the way we hope they will, even if our stories this side of heaven fall short of happily ever after.

"You will grieve," Jesus told his disciples, predicting their response when they realized it wasn't God's plan for him to seize political power, "but your grief will suddenly turn to wonderful joy.... I have told you all this so that you may have peace in me. Here on earth you will have many trials and sorrows. But take heart, because I have overcome the world" (John 16:20, 33). Because we serve a great God, we can find strength to trust that his goodness will win out, somehow, someway, sometime.

FOR REFLECTION

1. Have you ever risked something important to you and then experienced a disappointing result?

2. How did the disappointment or grief look when you were in the thick of it? How does it look to you today? How has the experience affected the way you think about dreams, risks, God, and faith?

3. Does it take more courage to follow a dream or let go of a dream? Do you believe God might want to transform your dreams into something new?

4. What is "the dawn of a morning of hope" for you? What risks are you willing to take to reach out for it?

Six
_____

REINVENTING

*It's Thursday. You can quit anything on a Thursday. Quit
believing the lie that your worst mistake defines who you are.*

Bob Goff, Twitter post

"No one likes a quitter," my dad used to say to us kids. I wanted
to be liked. Being liked was and often is my primary desire. So
quitting, if it makes people dislike me, is something I don't do. In
fact, if you tell me to quit something, I'll probably do the opposite.
You might even say I'm a tiny bit stubborn.

But I needed to quit my job at the treatment center. Therapy
was making that clear. How could I do it? I passionately loved
this job and the people I met through it. It was a privilege to play
an important role in the lives of patients who grew and changed.
It was a job I was meant to do despite the pain and sorrow that
came with the territory. I had watched so many people succumb to
mental illness and addiction.

Several factors contributed to the state I found myself in, but one issue I could no longer ignore was that the job had started to tear me apart. My body gave me plenty of warning signs, but I continued to do the work. I was increasingly frustrated that no one was fixing the problems I had clearly expressed to them. There was not enough staff and not enough staff support in crisis situations, and my only time away from patient care was when I hid away in a bathroom stall for quiet. I told management what I needed from them, yet I continued to do the work myself. Of course, why would they fix anything when I continued to step in and do it anyway? I made it look like it was all okay and it was all worked out. This pressing on despite the unrest inside me and the toll on my body was a repeated pattern throughout my life.

Going into therapy pulled back the curtain and exposed some things I hadn't previously been willing to look at. Like the fact that my job and I had become codependent.

One night in my kitchen, my three sons were rushing about and all I wanted to do was go to bed. My head hurt and I sat like a limp doll on the couch.

My ten-year-old stopped his frantic search for his shoes to look at me with his dark brown eyes under long eyelashes. "Mom," he said, "you're always so tired. You always have a headache. It's no fun."

Oh yes, buddy, you are so right. My heart ached in the face of the truth he could so clearly see. But what was I supposed to do about it?

Right around this time, I met Cara.

Cara is a fun-loving, extroverted, and energetic youth director who just had her first baby and is on maternity leave. She's been writing for years and longs for time to write a book. She says to whoever will listen that her dream has always been to speak and write full time. She just doesn't really believe it's possible. Certainly not right after having a baby.

Two weeks before she's set to return to her office, her boss, Jake, calls her.

"Cara, there's a problem," he says. "We've run out of money. I know you're on maternity leave, but some major decisions need to be made. And you have to be the one to make them."

Finances for her full-time ministry job are in the red. This means that until the ministry can get in the black again, she'll be reduced to 75 percent pay the first month and 50 percent pay the second month.

But it isn't just finances that have gone awry. In the course of her brief absence, board members resigned and the board chair became nonresponsive to both Cara and Jake. In her new-mom fog she can't put her finger on the cause of these problems. She can't understand why things have gone south in such a short amount of time. Why do key players on the donor board seem to be dropping like flies? Why have their financial sponsorships fallen off? She has no idea that things will get worse before they get better. Relationships begin to splinter.

She knows that as the mother of a newborn she won't be able to meet all the demands of directing a nonprofit organization as easily as before, but she wants to try. Before her leave is over, she resumes her work from home. She slowly eases herself back into the rhythm of responding to work emails and making phone calls, overwhelmed by the kinds of repairs she needs to make.

A week later she receives an email that changes her. The message is from a man named Sam. Sam is in the field of publishing and is interested in her writing.

Cara sits on her couch, breast milk and spit-up stains running down her clothes like a bad ombré-coloring job. She stares at his words. Tears of gratitude and hope form in her eyes.

But she stays at her job, tossing this opportunity aside for later. She stays because she loves the people and because she believes in the mission.

She starts to realize there are other reasons she stays, maybe less noble reasons. She stays because she legitimately likes being the person in charge—she likes the glittery crown she gets to wear almost every day. And maybe she stays because she's afraid of change, afraid of not knowing what will happen if she steps out of her familiar role. She stays because she doesn't think she has any other choice, because she fears it's too late to leave, because she has no idea how to start over. After almost a decade in full-time paid ministry, she doesn't know how to be someone else. Her identity is wrapped up in what she's got right now.

When she's honest with herself, she knows that feeding the flock isn't feeding her soul anymore. "I have been starving for too long," she tells me, "and Sam's email feels like the first drop of water I have tasted in a long, long time."

In *Strengthening the Soul of Your Leadership*, spiritual director Ruth Haley Barton wrote, "Such moments come to all of us— moments when our leadership feels like something we 'put on' like a piece of clothing pulled out of the closet for a particular occasion rather than something that flows from a deep inner well fed by a pure source."[1]

Though she doesn't launch herself into a new life right away, Sam's email is a springboard. She tests it, believing for the first time she might have a legitimate dream after all.

She meets with Sam at the end of her maternity leave. They eat croissants and drink coffee and talk shop at a tucked-away spot in an unassuming, quaint town. The encounter sparks something in her. Sam, who barely knows her as a person, believes in her words. His confidence encourages and empowers her to trust that this just might be the path she is supposed to follow. Still, she doesn't make a decision yet because she is unsure if she can leave her job. The risk is too great. So she returns to her job as youth director.

Just like that, her days of wearing yoga pants and fleece jackets are over. It's time for "us" to return to work. And this "us" is no problem to the organization she serves. Babies come along with the female staff and are welcome. Their family-friendly policies help Cara transition back into her responsibilities. Ten-week-old Canon begins journeying with Cara everywhere: to the office, to the local high school for student tutoring, to Nini's Coffee

Shop for ten o'clock breakfast meetings with college students. She builds her schedule around Canon, knowing when he'll fall asleep and when he'll need to be fed. She knows when he might need some time rolling around on the blanket on the office floor, just as she knows when he's had enough, when it is time to pack everything up and call it quits. He's her constant companion. He sees Cara try to do it all and be it all and lead them all. She is utterly exhausted by the end of the first week.

She is a full-time mom and a full-time director. She is a wife, even though she feels lacking in that area these days. She is a friend, even though she sometimes wonders if she'll ever see her girlfriends again, given the insanity of the schedule she now keeps.

Cara starts to doubt herself. *How do other women in my position continue working at this pace? Is this the curse of the working mom, that we're stretched so thin we have nothing to give to anyone else, let alone ourselves?*

The truth quickly presents itself to her. She knows within a week of going back to work that she can't sustain this pace with her health intact. She yearns for life. She wants to follow her dream, and she wants to have balance. She knows it's time to quit and pursue a vocation that allows her to be her son's primary caregiver while still serving the world through her words and stories.

It's time to pursue a different path.

Overwhelmed by the prospect of leaving her job, she's terri-fied to actually do it. But she sits in Jake's office and says, "I can't do this anymore; I really can't." Jake sits across from her, tears in the wrinkly corners of his eyes as he listens. When she's finished, he talks about what they can do to make it better. He tries to convince her to stay.

"Just get me out," she whispers, interrupting him. She's done.

Her resignation is public a month or so later, and an air of unforeseen, unknown change permeates her every conversation. "The core of my identity remains a wild beast in need of severe domestication," she confesses, "because my definition of self correlates entirely to my vocation. Leaving ministry also means I am about to wave a final farewell to everything I know how to be and do. And the unknown can be rather daunting, to say the least."

She admits she doesn't have the slightest clue how to make the writerly life happen, except by starting to write and getting the words out there. Is it even possible, with her infant son still in tow? What will her everyday life look like?

The annual Christmas party is also her good-bye party. Her colleagues share memories and shed tears. She cries too, both sad and afraid. Is she making a mistake? Still, it's time. She knows it's time, even though her heart mourns the loss of the people she has worked alongside for so long.

They gather in a festively adorned living room, holiday lights twinkling in the background while the smell of fresh Douglas fir tickles their noses. Canon squawks in the arms of her friends, and her husband, James, sits to her left, his steady hand placed on her back in comfort. They do that thing Christians have done since the days of the early church. Cara sits in a worn wooden chair in the center of the room. Those closest to her place hands on her shoulders, her arms, her knees. Those who can't reach her extend their hands, sending Spirit-driven energy from one body to the next to the next. They pray for Cara and thank God for her. They ask for blessings, pray that she might be a blessing, and send her off in peace.

"It is the holiest of moments. It is the hardest of nights," Cara says.

She turns in her keys two weeks later and heaves a sigh of anticipated relief. Come what may, a new journey lies ahead, whether she is ready for it or not.

My job was my calling. I was working in my own mission field, and I didn't want to leave it. But this perfect life was starting to wake me up at night, pounding me with migraines and forcing me to sleep much more than I needed.

For a while I was frustrated with my therapist and disappointed in my body. It was betraying me, failing to hold up under the pressures of this career I had worked so hard for. I wanted to stay where I was comfortable. At age forty-three, I didn't want to reinvent myself.

One day after work, I headed out for a run in the sweltering heat. With my headphones on and my feet pounding the hot pavement, I listened to Hillsong United's "Oceans."

You call me out upon the waters
The great unknown where feet may fail
And there I find You in the mystery.[2]

These words penetrated my stubbornness. I felt certainty then and knew as much as it is possible to know that I had to step out of my boat and trust. It was the right thing to do. The problem was my income was not optional for my family. Quitting wasn't a luxury we could afford. But my husband and I had many discussions, and he agreed it was the next right step.

So I quit. On a Thursday.

I walked into my boss's office, trembling, and sat on her couch. Would she hate me, yell at me, tell me what a horrible employee I was?

My words were almost identical to Cara's. "I can't do this anymore."

I was so scared and so worried about what everyone would say. But my supervisor looked at me, and you know what she did? She cried. She wept sweet tears of understanding. For me. It made me even more uncomfortable, but she was so supportive, so kind, and I was shocked.

I had jumped out of the boat, expecting to drown. Instead, she threw me a life vest. "Stay as long as you need, Lee. We will do whatever you need."

Even now I think, *How did this happen?*

We talked for a while, we hugged, and I walked away stunned.

This was right.

I had no idea where I was going. No idea what I would do. I was surely too old to find a new career that would give me as much joy as this one had.

My mind returned to the words of "Oceans."

I decided to trust. Trust that God had a plan.

To reinvent myself, I had to quit. Are reinventing and quitting the same thing?

I don't think so. To reinvent ourselves is to change for the better. To get healthier. To step out in bravery, following our dreams and passions. To not let comfort and routine be the stories of our lives.

As simple as it might seem on paper, change is hard, even scary. I wasn't sure if I was going about things the right way. I was just trying to take the right next step.

Eventually I was hired by a different treatment center, this time to do work that didn't directly involve patients. Three days into this new job, I received a phone call with the news that a publisher wanted this book you now hold. There was no way I could have written the book while working in the role I was in before.

God's timing was at work yet again. So perfect. So right.

When you feel a stirring and aching sense that something needs to change, take courage. Step out of your comfortable boat and learn to walk on water. Trust that you won't drown. Keep your eyes on the bigger story. This is the path to new growth and great adventure.

FOR REFLECTION

1. Is there something you need to quit in your own life? A habit, a belief, a job, or maybe even a relationship? What indicators make you think that now might be the right time for change?

2. Does the word *quitting* carry a negative meaning for you? Name some of the positive aspects of this word. What does it mean to *reinvent* something in our lives?

3. When you think about stepping out of your familiar boat, what fears keep your feet rooted? How could you overcome these fears and make choices anchored in trust instead?

4. Who could help you think through the decisions you want to make? Make yourself a promise to approach this person and ask for his or her wisdom.

Seven

FORGIVING

*As far as the east is from the west, so far has he
removed our transgressions from us.*

Psalm 103:12 (NIV)

When my first book finally found its place on the shelves at Barnes
& Noble, I spent many lingering moments in the corner of the
bookstore staring at it. *There it is!* I said quietly to myself. *There it
is!* And to the right of the single copy of my book sat ten copies
of the *New York Times* bestseller *Pastrix* by Nadia Bolz-Weber.
Because of the alphabetical arrangement, her books sat next to
mine.

I saw it and thought, *Hey, at least I'm next to a bestselling author.
Maybe that will help me sell some books.*

In time I read *Pastrix*. I thought it was amazing. I thought
Nadia was amazing. I became intrigued by this Lutheran pastor
who has tattoos up and down her arms and speaks in the kind

of raw language I became accustomed to during my work with addicts. So when I had the chance to hear her deliver the keynote address at a writing conference, I filed into a college gymnasium with three thousand others, eager to hear what she had to say. I wasn't going to miss this talk.

This chapter is not about the right and wrong ways to interpret Scripture or live a Christian life. I'm not going to comment here on whether Christians should swear. That's what people hone in on when someone who calls herself Christian behaves differently from how we think she should. I can say this because I'm guilty of passing this kind of judgment.

See, this chapter is about forgiving. It's my most challenging verb. This is the chapter I avoided writing.

There have been countless books written on the importance of forgiving others. If Jesus laid his life down to forgive all our sins, the least we can do is forgive others. "Forgiveness is a big deal to Jesus," Nadia wrote in *Pastrix*, "and like that guy in high school with a garage band, he talks about it, like, all the time."[1]

Throughout the process of writing this book, I interviewed many brave women who told incredible stories of what they learned about forgiveness and how they managed to do it. One wife's marriage was destroyed by her husband's affair. Another woman's husband committed suicide when she was six months pregnant. And another woman whose father abandoned her and her siblings when they were young.

Though I kept trying to write their stories of forgiveness, it became clear to me that what I really needed to write about was my own struggle and fear of this word *forgive* and my own questions about forgiving *myself*. What in my life needs forgiving? And if I forgive myself, if I stop feeling bad about myself, what will motivate me to keep becoming a better person?

We will come back to those questions. Right now, I want to introduce you to the woman who sits next to me in the gymnasium, listening to Nadia Bolz-Weber's bold words.

Carolyn is the definition of *class* and *confidence*. She's a stunning seventy-nine-year-old with perfect lipstick and elegant gray hair. Carolyn and I are both in the same writers' guild, and I finally met her in person at a writers' conference. (I know way more about this stranger than I should because I stalked her on Facebook.)

I know she was a judge in Washington, DC. I know her husband worked for the Secret Service. I know she is a Christian. And based on this scant evidence, I create a story in my head about what she must think of Nadia. I imagine her making discreet *tsk-tsk* sounds when Nadia shows up with all those tattoos and starts swearing.

Maybe I build these walls and put people in these categories in order to make sense of my world. Nadia fits into a couple of categories: recovering addict, reformed Lutheran female pastor. Carolyn fits into another: judge. *I wonder if she is a Democrat*, I think. *I wonder if she drives a Subaru.* See how I do it? See how

I compartmentalize people into little boxes? See how I come up with these stories as if I actually know these people?

Carolyn interrupts my thoughts. She leans over to me and says, "Nadia is my people."

I don't understand. How are she and Nadia anything alike? Carolyn with her fancy clothing and perfectly styled hair, Nadia with her punk-rocker look and combat boots. It turns out this former judge is nothing like what I imagined.

Her life as a judge sometimes would get lonely, she tells me as we get to know each other. She was well respected as an authority in the halls of the courthouse, but very few colleagues showed interest in her personal life. She missed her easy camaraderie with former lawyer colleagues. "I wouldn't be invited for lunch," she says, "because lawyers didn't want to be accused of trying to sway me or wanting something from me. And many were afraid of me. I could feel it."

In 1989 Carolyn found true acceptance and belonging at a most unlikely place when she and her husband started volunteering at a home for men with AIDS.

"Can you change a grown man's diaper?" the Mother Superior at the HIV shelter asked Carolyn during her interview.

"Well, I've changed my kids' diapers, but I don't know if I can do it on grown men. I'll try," she answered.

That was enough for the nun.

When she walked through the doors of the decrepit building, Carolyn shed her respected role and let the men there see who she was apart from her judge's robes. Here, no one knew she was a judge. For the first time in a long time, Carolyn felt accepted. Accepted for simply being who she was, a person who is loved by God and who has learned how to love back. The first time she walked into the room filled with men covered in bedsores and grasping at life, she sensed she was known.

"Were you scared?" I ask.

"If you mean was I scared of catching AIDS, yes. I was. Back then there was a hysteria about how easy it was to contract it. Plus, all day we were around bodily fluids from these men. I knew there was great risk."

But the experience radically changed her life. Carolyn quickly learned the art of loving these men rejected by society. Her job was to stay out of the way until someone yelled "volunteer," at which point she and her husband would quickly respond.

She tells me about a dying man, a memory that has stayed with her all these years.

As she and her husband worked to change the patient's soiled diaper, Carolyn nearly fainted when she saw the oozing sores covering his bottom. She could see how bad his plight really was. She wanted to help. They wanted him to know before he died that God loved him.

Her husband reached out and grabbed his hand and said, "God loves you."

The patient looked intensely at them both and said, "I love *you* too."

"This moment," Carolyn says to me, remembering. "*This moment*. My husband and I both felt in the deepest places of our souls that it wasn't this man saying, 'I love you too.' It was God saying it through him. It changed my life forever."

When I ask this beautiful woman what she thinks beauty is, she says, "I believe beauty is being able to see God in people. Even if you don't like them, if you look and see God created them, they have worth. They matter. Working in the AIDS shelter taught me this. Now I look for it in all people."

"Do you feel that what you did was brave?" I ask.

"Did I worry I was going to die? Yes. But I don't regret any of it for a minute. Most of the time when we are doing brave things, we don't know it at the time. But if we look close enough, God always shows up."

Nadia stands on the stage, convicting me of my judgments just by being herself. Carolyn straightens to listen, having shattered all my false notions of who she is. I'm filled with the pure truth that can come only from God working through someone else—someone unlikely, unexpected.

And I am shattered. I am here in the presence of not one but two of God's amazing women, who are placed in my life at this moment to teach me a valuable lesson about loving. And I know that if I had kept up my ridiculous assumptions, I would have missed all God had in store for me in that moment.

I wonder how many God encounters I've actually missed because of my own misguided judgments.

If we think God doesn't arrange our lives in a miraculous way like a beautiful and colorful quilt, we're in denial. We forget he does this. At least I do.

I need forgiveness daily. I need it for thinking I know what people are like based on how they look. I need it for the walls I build when I make assumptions about others. I need it for thinking I know how I'm supposed to be and for not embracing who God created me to be.

The week after the writing conference is over, I attend church. Not the building our family visits on Sunday mornings but our "home church," which meets once a month on a Sunday evening in someone's home. We're a vagabond group of family and friends who live all over the Twin Cities.

This group started years ago. When my oldest child was a baby, our family started going to family camp at the Castaway Club in Minnesota. A long weekend in the beautiful northern lakes region at this Young Life camp was just what we needed to restore our souls and prepare for the fall and long Minnesota winter. Summer after summer we'd make the drive to Detroit Lakes, stay in cabins, play the silly Young Life games, and relax in hammocks on the beach. This restorative weekend became a tradition not just for our family but for many of our friends. Then one year, about fourteen couples who met there every summer decided to make our gatherings a monthly habit as well.

No matter which home we meet in, this group of people represents one place in the world where I am known. This is where I am loved. Here, with these people, is where I know that all is right with the world.

But tonight I'm angry with myself. On this night in someone else's basement, my friend Angie plays her guitar, and I listen to everyone sing, mostly off-key, while I try to sort out this stirring of emotions that has me agitated.

Our friend Eric stands up to ask for prayer requests, and one of the little boys says, "That my friend would forgive me for being mean to him at recess."

Okay, okay. Forgiveness. Yes, God. Teach me.

I need this.

Eric stands up again after the prayers and tells a lively story of a time when he was very afraid. His arms are moving about and his expression is theatrical. He knows the Young Life motto "It's a sin to bore a kid with the gospel." The children and parents sit intrigued by his story. He pulls out his small black Bible and reads the Scriptures. Then Angie stands up with her guitar while the children pass around a little battery-operated candle. The lights go off and the voices of children and adults sing "Silent Night."

We're praising God elbow to elbow and knee to knee. I feel the sense of home. Of family. My faith was born through the transforming ministry of Young Life. And now, some thirty years later, when I get to praise God and laugh and love with these amazing and supportive families, I believe I know what heaven will feel like.

I feel love move over my imperfections. I feel my anger toward myself slipping away. I let go of the condemnation, the silly game I play: *If I could just be better … if I could just be good enough … God would really love me. Then I would be okay.*

Because in this crowded basement I know he loves me. I am okay, right now. It's impossible to believe anything else.

I remember something Nadia said that night as I sat next to Carolyn: "Our brokenness and our imperfections are the spaces where we stand in need of God in a way that we don't in our excellence."[2]

When I return home, I write this prayer of forgiveness because I realize I'll encounter God in my broken places if I allow him to go there.

> *Father in heaven, your name is bigger than anything I can understand. Can you help me? Can you help me understand that you aren't mad at me for judging people, you aren't mad at me for putting people in categories and making them fit in the mold I want them to? Father, can you forgive me and all of us here on earth for spending so much time like little junior high kids playing kickball, saying who is in and who is out, who is good and who is not? Can you forgive me for thinking that my will is best? I need forgiveness in my jealousy of that woman and her fancy yoga clothes, thinking she has it better than me or that my life would be complete if I lived in a house like hers. I need forgiveness in my piety, thinking that just because I don't swear, I*

am better than someone else. Help me to forgive the people who made me angry and who didn't offer me what I needed, and help me to forgive those who hurt me. Lead me not into the land of walls and religiosity but into a country where I can be like Carolyn and Nadia and live out of the bountiful blessing of love and forgiveness that you offered all of us on the cross. For you are the God who sees me, the God who searches for me, the God who created me and everyone else. Thank you for forgiving me again when I put my foot in my mouth and when I yell at my kids. Thank you for allowing me time on this earth to struggle. Thank you for surrounding me with others who teach me love and forgiveness.

And I hear the Lord say in reply, "Come now, let us settle the matter.… Though your sins are like scarlet, they shall be as white as snow; though they are red as crimson, they shall be like wool" (Isa. 1:18 NIV).

Amen.

FOR REFLECTION

1. Why do you think it is particularly difficult to forgive ourselves?

2. What might *not* forgiving yourself gain you? For example, maybe you believe beating yourself up helps keep your behavior or pride

in check. Is this thing you gain greater than the unconditional love Jesus offers us through his total forgiveness?

3. It is easy to fall into a pattern of judging others. What habitual patterns do you struggle to overcome? Is it possible for you to believe God continues to love you despite these struggles?

4. Who are the people in your life who surround you with the confidence that you are a beloved child of God? If you don't know such people, where might you find them? How could you be such a person in someone else's life?

Eight

SEPARATING

The way we talk to our children becomes their inner voice.

Peggy O'Mara

Mother, Mom, Mommy.

Those words whisper to me from the colorful and flower-filled greeting cards staring back at me. Cards that carry sentiments such as "Thank you for being there for me. Thank you for being my best friend."

Kind, loving, and tender cards written to mothers for Mother's Day.

Where, then, is the card that tells my story? The story about the mother who wasn't mothered well and never learned to do it well herself. The story about the generations of verbal abuse and cutting remarks masked as love.

I know I'm not alone.

As she prepares to walk down the aisle to the love of her life, Kristen can't get her mother's words out of her head, words spoken over her since she was a little girl.

"No guy will ever be able to put up with you. You're so hard to please."

The message joins so many others, always in the back of her mind.

Her mother says to Kristen's fiancé, "We can't believe you stick with her. She's so hard to live with."

Maybe this would make sense if Kristen had been a teen rebel or a difficult and challenging child, even though it wouldn't make it more acceptable. But Kristen is just the opposite. She is kind, tender, and one of the most caring people I know. But her road to separating from her mother, who has been clinically diagnosed with narcissism, has been a rocky and challenging path.

Before the wedding Kristen has an issue with her fiancé's sister. She meets her mom for lunch and shares the situation with her. Instead of helping her sort things out, Diane says, "I don't think you should marry him. This will only get worse."

Kristen says nothing but listens as she always does.

Her mom continues, "I think you're going to have lots of problems and he'll choose his family over you. His mom and sister are crazy, and you'll never be happy."

Diane says this as if it's truth, and Kristen falls yet again under her spell.

She does what she has always done. She doesn't argue; she wants to honor her mother. She wants to be the good girl and not make waves. She still longs for her mother's love and approval, even as a grown woman. Only when she's away from her mom and shares the story with her fiancé and friends does she see the truth. What Kristen slowly begins to realize is that the happier she gets, the more deflated Diane is.

The wedding is another typical experience of disappointment for Kristen. She waits alone in the back room while her stylist does her hair. She is still that little girl longing for her mother to approve, nurture, and love. But her mom doesn't come and tell her how beautiful she looks or how proud she is of her. Her mom is nowhere to be seen. Her parents are more concerned with the dog they left in the hotel room—the dog Kristen has clearly stated may not be part of the wedding. And yet after the wedding ceremony is over, they bring the dog to the reception.

Then she doesn't hear from them for months, another disappointment piled among the many, stacked like boxes over the years.

It's time to speak up. Time for Kristen's voice to be heard. Time to name the problem.

Alison also yearns for approval from her parents. She's forty years old and still carries with her the ingrained message that it's her responsibility to care for them. Never mind the fact that she's never enough, a disappointment they remind her of often. She exhausts herself by inviting them to everything, talking to their doctors when there is an emergency, hosting all the holidays, and carrying the burden of their future care while raising her own four daughters. She wants to be a good daughter, but mostly she just wants them to love her. Her needs and desires are always second to theirs. Because of the rigid Christian faith that clouded her life, she grew to believe that nothing but total obedience was acceptable. Anything else would result in verbal or physical abuse.

Alison is in her kitchen when her life flips upside down. Her dad has phoned to say he and her mother are coming over with news. Alison thinks it's an illness or a financial disaster. She can't fathom the words that will be spoken to her when they arrive and take a seat at her table.

"Alison," her aging father says with his back slumped and his hands in his lap, "about ten years ago I touched a girl in an inappropriate way, and I need to tell you about it."

She swallows and stares at him. He continues, "I need to tell you about it because the girl told the police and I've had to go to court. It's coming out now because the girl was under the age of twelve when this happened."

Alison looks at her mom, who's staring down at the ground. Hot anger pumps through her blood as she watches her mom fold into herself and weaken at the words.

Her eyes feel heavy and her heart races. Why did they wait until she was alone to tell her this?

A thought passes through her mind and her stomach sinks. *My daughters … were my daughters victims?* But she quickly changes gears to focus on helping her parents, always helping. She tries to think of her role, of some way to be the honorable daughter through this.

She tries to remain calm as she senses the familiar tug. *They want something from me.* It's an irresistible pull of obligation. She wants them to stop dumping on her but continues to let them.

She turns back to her dad and tries to figure out who the little girl was and when the crime happened. He begins to cry and wring his hands in nervous fear. "I've hurt your mother," he says, sobbing. "I've been unfaithful to her."

Alison's mind is like a fire truck with every thought loud and ear-piercing. How could he equate molesting a girl with being unfaithful to her mom? How could she be hearing this?

"Wait, Dad, how long did this go on?" she asks.

"This little girl, she sat on my lap," he says. "She wiggled around in a way that seduced me."

Alison begins to go numb. Questions dance in her mind, but the rest of her body tunes out.

"I was powerless to resist and had asked God to help me. But I couldn't stop because she kept coming on to me." Somehow this all made sense to him.

Her mom has twisted a wadded Kleenex around her finger. She places her hand on Alison's arm and squeezes it in a firm grip.

"You cannot tell your brothers and sister about this," she says with her mouth set hard.

The secret keeper. The caretaker. Until this moment, Alison has found her identity in all the roles she's had to play. They make her feel important in this family.

"Dad will have a monitoring device put around his ankle for five months. So that means we can't come over to your house until the authorities take it off. You will just have to come to our house." Her mother announces this with a small shake in her voice.

It's clear what is happening here. They want to act as if nothing happened, as if everything is normal. If Alison can buy the lie they're selling, it will help them believe it too—that nothing has changed.

But *everything* has changed. Scenes from her life begin to flash in front of her, times when she maybe saw the clues. What if this happened earlier than just the time he was caught? She has no idea how to sort through it all. Then she thinks of her daughters—how will she protect her daughters? Her mind is racing. Still, she doesn't want to disobey her parents or show her anger. She stands frozen, unsure what is the right thing to do.

The room is quiet. Alison stands, looking at her kitchen, her home, her house of love, now forever tainted with the memory of her dad telling her this story.

Without thinking, she takes on the mantle of the parent again. "You know, Dad, it isn't too late for you to change. You have a lot of things you need to face now. You both have a lot of work you need to do. Don't you see? God is giving you a second chance.

Come clean and learn from this situation. This is an opportunity, a reset button. A way to make all your relationships better before you die."

Alison falls back into her place as if it were a comfortable chair. She can even play the role of spiritual guide. And then she feels a sense of wrongness in all of it. Her parents are looking for her to rescue them. But it is *wrong*. She feels the error of this somewhere deep.

Inside her mind, her real voice is screaming at them, *What have you done? What are you going to do to make this better? You've disappointed me, and you've harmed a young girl!*

But she doesn't say those things. Instead, she ducks her head. Her role is to honor her parents, no matter what. She is terrified of standing up to them, terrified of displeasing God.

"How about we pray?" she says next.

Both women are confronted with a crossroads and a choice. How can they honor their parents when their parents are harming them?

At what point do we separate from our parents? When we are children, we have normal expectations and needs. If we don't receive what we need, especially if mental illness is present, we are at risk of spending our entire lives looking for fulfillment from people who aren't capable of offering it.

At what point do we put our hands up and say, "No more!"? Alison has four daughters, and she can't in good conscience allow her father to be around them. Kristen has to start making her life with her new husband.

What if honoring our parents doesn't mean blindly obeying them but instead means putting up boundaries and protecting ourselves and the next generation from abuse? I believe it does.

Setting safe boundaries is one of the bravest and hardest things we have to do as adults. I know because I have had to do this in my own life. Daring to set limits within a family system feels like ripping off one of your own limbs. It feels counterintuitive. We're more inclined to think, *They're my family—shouldn't I at least try to show them Christ's love?*

When I search for a Mother's Day card and when I'm on the phone listening to all the ways I need to be a better daughter, I'm reminded of this verse: "When I was a child, I spoke and thought and reasoned as a child. But when I grew up, I put away childish things" (1 Cor. 13:11).

While the verse is referring to how we live out our faith, I think it also applies to how I live out my relationships with people who continue to do harm. When I was a child, I didn't know anything different from being called a selfish, unloving little brat. I didn't have the tools or the ability to speak up. But as an adult I do.

I checked in with my good friend and trauma therapist Felicia Snell to ask for her clinical insight into Kristen's and Alison's stories. At first she said, "I would tell these women to run as far away from these people as they can!"

We both laughed, knowing this would be ideal but isn't as realistic or as easy as it sounds. But then she said, "Narcissistic parents know no boundaries. They believe everything a[t] more important than anyone else, including th[e] Setting personal boundaries can change your life people are allowed to treat you. Boundaries pr[o ... the] framework for you to be responsible for your own feelings and needs and release you from taking on the responsibilities of carrying the burden of your parents' life, moods, feelings, and distorted perceptions."[1]

When it comes to distorted perceptions, the way such parents project self-worth onto their children is devastating. "Children of narcissists emerge from this crucible with a common and most serious problem," wrote psychotherapist Elan Golomb in *Trapped in the Mirror*. "They feel they do not have the right to exist. Their selves have been twisted out of their natural shape since any movement toward independence is treated as a betrayal and something that can cause the parent irreparable harm."[2]

The truth, of course, is that children are the ones harmed by the behavior of the parents.

Many women are faced with making very difficult choices about their family members and other significant people in their lives. When are we going to learn it's okay to stand up for what's right and true, beginning with the fact that we are valuable? We are loved by a perfect Father who has planned an eternity full of love for us. In some situations, staying in an unhealthy relationship can keep us from fully experiencing the breadth of God's love. Only when we stop looking to a person for the love we want can we find it in a God who has an abundance to give.

Alison and Kristen protect themselves and their families in different ways.

Alison grieves the loss of the father she thought she knew. She suffers the pain of knowing the horrific things he did. It seems like it might be easy for her to put up a boundary, but it is horribly challenging. She sees a therapist and begins to do the trauma work that's needed to heal from her family's generational secrets. In time she sets extraordinarily rigid boundaries and cuts off all contact with her parents.

Kristen takes another path and hopes for change. She wants repair and resolution. Three years after the wedding, she calls a family meeting and asks for an apology. She wants her parents to acknowledge that their behavior hurt her.

When confronted, her mom acts like a wild animal that's been attacked. The claws come out. She says to Kristen, "You are cruel. And you lack compassion. The only person who makes you a better person is Craig. He's the only reason you're nice. Before Craig, you were the meanest person I've ever known."

Kristen freezes in her chair and silently weeps. She is still just a little girl longing for her mommy to love her.

Diane says, "I love you because I'm your mom, but I don't really like anything about you. I haven't liked anything about you for a long time." Her dad sits silent, his arm around her mom in solidarity and submission to whatever she says.

After this encounter with her mom, so much like the hundreds before, Kristen realizes she'll never receive the love she needs from Diane. Finally, with the help of her husband, therapist, and a group of loving friends, she shuts the door to her parents.

The boundary in the relationship has now been set by Kristen. The pain and years of abuse are taking time and work to overcome. But she is finally free to get out from under the shadow cast by her narcissistic mother.

She bounces through the stages of grief. First in denial and shock, her body reacts, and she starts having panic attacks. Prayer is her lifeline. Prayer, therapy, and her supportive friends.

God, let me know, she prays. *God, should I engage in this relationship again? God, I know they are human.* She knows all parents try to do the best they can with what they have. Her ability to see this in her parents makes her want to try again. But then she remembers all the times she has already tried.

She starts to let them go, and in letting go she begins to feel a closeness to God. He is her parent, and he provides her with other people who take care of her. She is grateful. She clings to them for support.

"Since I have made the decision to have no contact with them, God has truly increased my friendships, the quality of my relationships, and my ability to be vulnerable with my friends and husband. Now I can be honest and accept feedback," she explains. "The feedback is opposite from what I received from my parents. My friends and husband are loving, nurturing, and affirming."

But she still struggles with questions. Is she a bad person to give up on this relationship? Is she a bad person not to want to do it anymore?

"I was so ashamed of the story," Kristen says. "It is so heartbreaking to admit. My parents want nothing to do with me. They want no relationship with me. And to admit I am okay having parents who don't want to have contact with me—it is really hard to say that out loud."

Now she is living a healthy life with her husband, her friends, and her community. And during the day she helps kids through her work as a therapist.

"I think it is because my parents are so ill that I wanted to work with ill kids. I love being able to advocate for these kids who have very messy parents. It's wonderful to be able to stand up for them and say, 'This isn't appropriate,' and do it in ways that no one was able to do for me. Sometimes it is a little too much for me because I am still human and the separation still hurts. But God still has me doing this work with kids, so I will continue. I will keep seeing what his plan is, not my mom's. Only God's. And in that I am finding freedom."

We are born with an innate need for protection and love. It's intrinsic to how we are made. And when we don't receive what we need from our parents, where do we find it? How do we find our voice?

Some of us as adults continue to search for what we didn't get as children, and we can lose ourselves in the process. If we're not careful, we'll try to fill the gaping hole in our lives with empty accolades, possessions, or other pseudo-affirmations of our worth.

Only God can fill those broken places with enough love to overcome the anger and resentment. With the help of healthy people who are willing to walk with us through the work of grief, we can affirm our worth again and stop the generational cycle of abuse.

I've chosen a relationship with my own mother, but I do draw firm boundary lines. There are no Mother's Day cards that offer platitudes, but I look instead for the simple card that wishes her love instead of one that praises the mothering that didn't actually occur. When I ache for what I didn't have, I find Jesus sitting in a rocking chair where I can lay my head and be comforted and loved. He loves me as the child I was who was left empty and as the adult I am now who sets healthy and clear boundaries. It's challenging, and I mess up a lot. But trying is an important step of bravery.

FOR REFLECTION

1. This chapter is about adult children separating from their unhealthy parents, but the principles might apply to any unhealthy relationship. Did this chapter cause you to think of a relationship in your own life that might need boundaries?

2. How do you think the Christian principles of honoring your parents, loving your enemies, praying for those who hurt you, and similar commands apply to situations in which you or your family members are being hurt?

3. In what ways do you look to other people to fulfill your need for approval, belonging, self-worth, and nurturing? What would you need to do to make God the source of these important things?

4. What makes it hard for you to establish—or enforce—healthy boundaries in your own life? Who might be able to be your ally in this effort?

Nine

BELONGING

*I pulled you in from all over the world, called you in from every
dark corner of the earth, telling you, "You're my servant, serving
on my side. I've picked you. I haven't dropped you." Don't panic.
I'm with you. There's no need for fear for I'm your God. I'll give you
strength. I'll help you. I'll hold you steady, keep a firm grip on you.*

Isaiah 41:8–10 (THE MESSAGE)

Most of the kids on the playground in this Minnesota town have
blond hair and blue eyes. Not all, but most. When fair-skinned
kids taunt Sarah with the word *Chink* or walk by and pull at the
corners of their eyes to make them slanted, she doesn't understand
why they're making fun of her.

Because as far as she knows, she looks just like them. Even
though she doesn't. Sarah is Vietnamese and was adopted at age
four into a loving Christian family of four blond-haired, blue-
eyed sisters and brothers. She is one of them. They're her family.

And she believes in every part of her mind and heart that she looks just like them.

When she looks in the mirror, she sees a white girl with blonde hair.

This sounds baffling, doesn't it? How could Sarah not see herself as she is? How could she not see the darker tones of her skin and hair? How could she not see in the family photo that she's different?

I suspect that to varying degrees we all try to imagine and make ourselves into what we think the world wants us to be. I get it.

I wanted to be quiet because I was told I was too loud. I wanted to be thin because I was told I was fat. These messages became so ingrained in my mind that in my early twenties I unconsciously began to lose myself in the process of making myself belong. In the mirror I saw fat where there were only bones, and in the world I saw a boisterous girl who needed to be silenced. Each day my real self died a little bit inside, until the day I almost died physically.

Sarah doesn't see the person God made her to be until she's in high school, when the mirage clouding her eyes begins to fade. Standing in the hallway of her school, she sees them: the pretty blonde girls holding hands with the boys, the white couple at the football game kissing in the stands. The pretty girls with the glistening yellow hair are the ones who go out on dates, who get invited to prom, who lead the way. She stands at her locker and begins to see and feel her differences. *I'm not like them. I'm not like any of them. Where do I belong?*

Her parents never push her to be someone she isn't. They affirm her heritage. They encourage her to attend camps and groups where she can meet other Vietnamese people. But she won't do it. She has nothing in common with them, she thinks. Admitting she is different—embracing the person God made her to be—might make her stand out, might make her not belong.

Sarah marries Joe, a Caucasian man. As she gets older, she begins to see and accept herself as the Vietnamese person she is. As much as she's able.

Until she and Joe travel to Vietnam.

They spend the first part of the trip on the sandy beaches of Da Nang, the city where Sarah spent her first four years in an orphanage. Her father died in the war and her mother died in childbirth, and all Sarah knows of her early life is an address written on a piece of paper.

The city is filled with spectacular buildings and beautiful bridges. Joe and Sarah rent scooters and ride around, exploring the city. Near the place where the orphanage is supposed to be, they find a parking place just big enough for their scooters. They park, hop off, and decide to ask a wrinkled old man at a trinket stand for directions. His name is Le Wyn, and he's kind and welcoming to Sarah and Joe. Sarah hands him the piece of paper, and in his broken English he says, "Oh, I know where this is!"

It isn't far. He walks them to the building where Sarah's life began. The run-down old building is now a home for Catholic nuns. Le Wyn introduces them to his daughter, who works there and also speaks English. They see the building and walk through a few rooms. Le Wyn tells them, "During the war, the North take over everything. They make all the children leave the orphanage. They burn all the papers."

Sarah believes this is the end of her story, but before she leaves she gives Le Wyn her contact information, just in case he or his daughter ever come upon anything.

After Sarah and Joe say good-bye, Le Wyn's daughter spreads the word about a beautiful Vietnamese woman who came to visit the orphanage. She has a friend who grew up in the same orphanage, a friend who is still in contact with those who operated it. Le Wyn's daughter tells him of the connection, and he calls Sarah at her hotel and says, "The people who ran the orphanage are still alive. They now have a church in Da Nang and we would take you there."

"Of course!" Sarah says. "I would love that."

She meets Pastor Hut, and he embraces her as if she were a long-lost child. His wife and other women from the church treat her as they would a fragile doll. They know who she is and even have a picture of her when she was a baby. They're overjoyed she has come, and they talk so fast in Vietnamese that she has no idea what they're saying, but it's clear they're thrilled to see her. She learns her name was My Lei.

Then Pastor Hut says, "I think a relative is looking for you!"

He explains that a few years earlier a man—an uncle or a brother—came around asking about her. "Do you know of this girl?" the man asked. But because there were no records, Pastor Hut had no information to offer.

Sarah knows she has no relatives. They all died in the war. She believes the pastor is mixing her up with someone else. But she enjoys her time with these resilient people and soaks up the beauty of her homeland. Soon she and Joe return to their lives in Minnesota.

In 2010 Sarah and Joe decide to go back. This time they take their son and daughter and Joe's parents. In Da Nang they visit Pastor Hut and Le Wyn. They enjoy their friendly smiles, their wrinkled, sun-soaked skin, and their warm hugs. They are Sarah's only living connection to Vietnam, and she treasures them. This time she also exchanges contact information with Pastor Hut so they can stay in touch.

In 2013 Sarah receives a strange email written in Vietnamese. She's ready to mark it as spam but then hesitates. Maybe it's from Pastor Hut. She decides to ask her foster brother, Cuong, whose Vietnamese family lives in Minnesota now, to translate it.

He does this and sends it back to her. The email reads, "Are you Sarah Huss? If you are Sarah Huss, I am your stepbrother, Tom. You have a brother and a sister who are looking for you. If you are her, please call this number."

Sarah is confused. She thinks it's a hoax. She doesn't have a brother. She doesn't have a sister.

She calls her mom. "I got this really weird email, and it says I have family in Vietnam!"

Her mom is confused too but advises her to see what it's about.

Cuong helps her. Together they call the number. The man on the other end is stunned beyond belief. He speaks Vietnamese, and Cuong translates for Sarah. He says, "I have been looking for you for more than forty years!"

His name is Hat. He's the oldest sibling in her family. He felt a responsibility to find her, to hold the family together. For many years he was on a television show that tried to help people find children who had been adopted out of the country. Every time he visited America, he asked agencies for their help locating her. He always came up empty.

Sarah is still confused.

"Why was I given up for adoption?" she asks. It's the first thing that comes to her mind. Why was she given up for adoption while he and her sister weren't?

Her newfound brother explains that Sarah was born in a small village in a remote jungle where homes were few and far between. She was the third child. Twenty days after Sarah's birth, their mom died. Their dad was at war. It was 1968, a critical time.

Sarah's aunt had also just given birth to a baby. The family didn't have formula, and though her aunt tried to breastfeed her, she couldn't produce enough milk for Sarah. The family went from neighbor to neighbor, looking for food for the baby, but no one had any.

Sarah's uncle asked the Americans for help. They told him of an orphanage in Da Nang that would take care of her. "When the war is over, you can go back and get her," they told him.

Her uncle and grandpa took her to the orphanage. And somehow in the chaos of it all, they didn't sign papers that said they intended to come back and get her. Instead, they signed papers to have her adopted. They were always under the impression they could return and retrieve Sarah. And so when Sarah's brother, Hat, came to look for her in 1975 after the war had ended, he learned Sarah had been sent to America. From that moment on, Hat felt he had let Sarah down.

Sarah has so many questions, but the language barrier presents a challenge.

Hat tells her their father returned from the war to find his wife had died and his baby was gone. He had never met Sarah.

Two months after this conversation with her biological brother, Sarah and her family, including one of Sarah's sisters and their mother, return to Vietnam. Her biological father is seventy-eight and diabetic. They're worried they won't have the chance to meet in person.

They meet Pastor Hut and Le Wyn, and their families go with her to meet Sarah's family. They must travel a considerable distance. Everyone who's been involved in her story for the past ten years comes together for this important moment. Sarah is overwhelmed.

When Sarah and her family arrive at her dad's house, the entire village comes out. She feels like a movie star. Well, a movie star who's sweating profusely in the stifling heat. It's the hottest time of the year in Vietnam—105 degrees Fahrenheit, 100 percent humidity, and no wind. It's hard to breathe or think. Her kids are miserable. She hopes the elderly Pastor Hut doesn't pass out.

She meets her father and siblings, and for the first time, she sees people who look like her—something she had longed for her entire life. Now she can see where she got her eyes and her smile. She and Hat bear a strong resemblance to each other.

Sarah finally sees herself as God sees her. She finally sees who she is, and she begins to accept and cherish it.

With a smile that stretches his face, Pastor Hut claps his hands together in pure absolute wonder and exclaims, "This is a miracle from God."

But when Sarah leaves Vietnam after meeting the family she never knew she had, a family and a community that had been praying for her return for all these years, she takes with her a deep sadness and confusing burden.

Sarah has no idea what to do with this new information. She can't communicate with them very well because of the language barrier. This gives her a deep sense of loss and uncertainty. She feels pulled between two different worlds.

Three years later Sarah is still processing her story. Her new story. This story of a little girl who was found but never knew she was lost.

"In my heart I ask, *What am I supposed to do with this? How is my relationship with them supposed to be?* My brother thought we would communicate all the time, but we live in two different worlds and the language barrier makes it so hard."

Her niece is learning English and communicates with her and sends her photos.

Her feelings about it fluctuate as she continues to try to wrap her head around all of it.

"Little did I know what was happening on the other side of the world throughout my life. I have never felt more special or more precious in the eyes of God because of the ways he so perfectly orchestrated this to happen. It is what amazes me to this day. Everything was orchestrated from the minute I met Joe to the minute we parked our scooters in front of Le Wyn's stand. We call Le Wyn my angel. And then, just from his daughter talking to a friend, everything unfolded exactly as God knew it would.

"It was such a blessing, so amazing. My kids got to meet their biological grandfather and aunt and uncle and blood cousins from my side and see where their Vietnamese characteristics come from. I got to meet my mom's brothers. I wish I could speak Vietnamese."

I think the journey to discovering our true identity is one we walk our whole lives. Our understanding doesn't always unfold in the time frame we'd like, but God is always at our side, urging us onward, holding us close to him.

I imagine God weeps when we try to be someone we are not and when we tell him who we are is unacceptable. We don't speak up because it's not okay to be seen as the one with questions. We try to change our appearance because we're dissatisfied with how we look. When I was little, I would watch quiet girls and wish to be like them because in trying to be like them, I wouldn't have to be me.

Sarah is an American with an important history in Vietnam; she's Vietnamese but can't speak the language of her biological family. Where does she fit in?

As far as the question relates to her cultural identity, the answer is still working itself out. But when it comes to her identity in Christ, the answer is clear: she belongs in the arms of the God who created her exactly as she was meant to be and put her in exactly the story he wants her to experience. If our desire to fit in causes us to turn our backs on the fact that we belong safely in God's arms, we might never experience a true sense of belonging.

God didn't make me quiet and demure, and he didn't make me to conform. He made me uniquely me, just as he made Sarah uniquely her. I know and believe it. I no longer try to be someone I'm not, and I can tell you for sure that not everyone likes the authentic me.

That's okay. Sarah doesn't pretend either. Today what she tells her children and helps other women try to embrace as well is this: "Be who God created you to be. He places value on you being you! It's okay to look or act different from other people. Just be yourself and be strong in who you are. Be strong in God."

I have found truly embracing who we are with all of our strengths and brokenness to be very freeing. When we each finally embrace this truth for ourselves, I believe God has a party and rejoices!

FOR REFLECTION

1. What are the qualities you dislike about yourself? How much of this dislike comes from your desire to have the approval of certain people (such as family members, peer groups, religious authorities, professional colleagues)?

2. Do you think any of these qualities need to change in order for God to accept and love you? Why or why not?

3. How has your personal story, the experiences of your life, shaped the way you think about what it means to truly belong?

4. Discuss some of the ways that having a secure sense of belonging in the arms of God is different from being seen as acceptable in the eyes of people.

Ten

ENDURING

*We may find relentless heartache in our days, but
our days must never lose relentless hope.*

Ann Voskamp, Twitter post

I'm embarrassed to hear myself say it. Embarrassed to even pray
this out loud: *Lord. Please, Lord. Don't make me a mom with the
balloons. Please, Lord.* It's a whispered prayer of utter desperation.

My seven-year-old son, Tommy, is in the basement with me.
We're trying to sleep on the pull-out couch while the bars poke
into our backs and musty, damp odors fill our lungs. His body
begins to twitch again next to mine, and I know it is happening.
I can tell by the fast spasms of his muscles, by his head that jerks
back and forth like he's telling his body *no* over and over again, and
by the little trickle of drool draining out of his mouth. I can't do
anything but watch and softly wipe the saliva off his cheek while
he has yet another seizure. His body and brain fill with palpable

electricity. Our first meeting with the neurologist isn't for a week, so until then I sleep with him, hoping to comfort him during these awful seizures.

That's when I think of the balloons: green ones and orange ones and purple ones. Balloons are a gesture of kindness in our community to support families when a child dies. This doesn't happen often, but often enough that everyone knows why. When a neighbor ties a single balloon onto a light post or a tree, you know: a child has gone too soon. And when I see them floating in the air, I want to drive away and I don't want to think about it. I know this loss could come to any of us. Life is so fragile, breath so fleeting.

Each night as I watch my youngest son's body seize and flail on the old mattress, I pray and remember. And I don't think it is right that I ask to be spared the balloons. I feel guilty and sad, and my heart aches. I remember the sound of my neighbor Zibby the day she found out her middle son had died suddenly. I remember it as if it happened only seconds ago, her rushing into the driveway with a phone in her hand. She had just received a call that her son Timmy had collapsed and died while hiking with the Boy Scouts in New Mexico. She began screaming a guttural scream that comes from a place so deep and so primal you can't help but buckle in pain hearing it. The sound of a mother who has lost her child. When I hear a sound so deep and painful like her cries, everything in me quivers.

Tommy is able to get help for his seizures, so I don't get those balloons. I'm full of relief. And questions. I can't explain why balloons went to Zibby and not to me.

When I began this journey of exploring women and bravery, the women who first came to mind were women like Zibby. Women who have lost children. I stood with Zibby the first day she returned to the bus stop, marveling at her courage and her ability to walk to the place where her little boy would never stand again. How could she put her feet on the ground each day and take steps forward?

At a fifth-grade graduation, I see Katey Taylor in the front row. She wears a pretty blue dress and sits with her long legs crossed. On her lap is the program bearing the list of children's names. I feel this guilt again. Her daughter was supposed to be in the sea of kids graduating. My son Matt, Tommy's older brother, is there, but her daughter isn't.

Katey is one of the bravest women I know.

Abbey Taylor is a fiery little spirit in a family of four girls. She has tiny freckles on each cheek and a huge love for anything sparkly and girly.

On a Friday in June 2007, seven-year-old Abbey is happily riding her scooter up and down the driveway. Her mom, Katey, yells out the door, "Hey, should we go to the pool?" Her four daughters shriek with excitement and scatter to gather their suits and towels. Soon the family is at the pool with friends, enjoying the beautiful late afternoon.

The smell of meat on the grill and sunblock fill the air. After the meal, they let the children go back in the pool for one more quick dip. Then all the girls hit the showers. Everyone but Abbey. She's still in the kiddie pool. Katey sees her sitting there and calls for her. When Abbey stands up to get out, it's clear something is wrong. She looks dizzy. She walks sideways a couple of steps. Then she topples over, hits her head on the pool deck, knocks out her front tooth, and falls with a loud splash into the adult pool.

Katey's heart drops and she rushes into action. *It's just sunstroke,* she thinks as she desperately pulls her little girl out of the pool. Someone calls 911. Abbey lies on the hard, warm pavement and drifts in and out of consciousness, her body limp and her eyes opening and closing. Katey is kneeling beside her little girl, stroking her wet hair, desperate for a sign of hope. Abbey comes to and groggily cries, "My stomach hurts. My stomach hurts."

Sirens and doctors swirl around them, and before Katey knows it she's at the hospital, her husband by her side as they run next to the gurney rolling down the cold hospital hallway. Katey holds Abbey's hand, avoiding the IV line, until Abbey is rolled into the surgery room for what the doctors say is a rectal tear. The large doors close, separating Katey and Scott from their little girl. Their little girl, who only hours ago was joyously riding her scooter.

They don't learn the horrifying truth of what actually occurred at the pool until after Abbey is out of surgery. A doctor with a somber face tells Katey and Scott, "Abbey has been disemboweled by the suction from an uncovered pool drain. It's hard to believe, but her small intestine has been ripped from her body. There is no medical reason why she has even survived this far."

But she is alive. And they are hopeful.

Her first surgery connects her stomach directly to her large intestine. Then she has her gallbladder and appendix removed. She experiences serious complications, including high fevers, internal bleeding, and infection. This is only the very beginning.

Katey anxiously waits at her daughter's bedside in the cold, sterile ICU. In the first few days, Katey tries to learn to live in this tiny room even though the sounds of the machines terrify her. But as time passes, the sounds become reassuring. A soothing pattern of beeps means Abbey's heart is beating. The sound of the pumps means she is breathing. The vibrating sound means fluid is being extracted from her lungs. Machines become the lullaby, assuring Katey her daughter is alive.

They find a way to make the children's hospital a home away from home. They befriend nurses and share gifts with other children on the floor. They try to make the best out of a horrific situation. Abbey's sisters and Katey decorate the walls with colorful drawings and letters from friends. Abbey fights like a tiny warrior.

"What does the future hold for Abbey?" Katey and Scott ask the doctors over and over. In the short term, the doctors hope to get her healthy enough to go home and get back to school. Discussions begin with the staff at a couple of transplant centers, and the family makes plans to visit them. Katey and Scott's greatest hope is for Abbey to heal and return to a normal, although different, life. But they must place all of it in God's hands.

While waiting for the transplant, Abbey does her best to return to life as a first grader. She's so excited to be back at school.

She runs across the playground, and other little girls happily flock around her. She's overjoyed to ride the bus and resume a life of kickball, girls' club, and playtime with friends.

Being in public is not as easy as it used to be, however. Abbey's skin is jaundiced, and the children at school constantly pepper her with questions. Initially, Abbey is quick to explain why her color is off, but she soon grows tired of explaining. The principal intervenes and helps rally the kids to understand what's happening to their friend. Abbey, full of strength, stands in front of her first-grade class and tells them how much it hurts her feelings to be treated differently. She asks them to think before they say something that could hurt someone else.

Katey and Scott have similar encounters. As Halloween approaches, people turn around and stare at Abbey. One woman stops and asks Katey at the grocery store, "How did you get her makeup like that? What did you use to color her eyes?" Katey politely replies, "She has a medical condition that causes the discoloration."

These are small matters next to the joy of having their daughter home again.

One question hums persistently in the back of everyone's minds: *Will she receive the transplants?* Katey and Scott have to battle multiple times with the insurance company to get them to pay for the cost of the transplants. They face mountains of paperwork and attend countless appointments and meetings. They tend to all the practical matters, but there is no guarantee the organs Abbey needs will ever become available.

Katey and Scott channel their frustration and impatience into helping support and pass the federal Pool and Spa Safety Act so other children will never experience what Abbey did. And they continue to pray fervently for the future of their child.

Katey focuses on her role as Abbey's cheerleader. She goes in search of hospitals and doctors who believe Abbey's complete recovery is possible. Katey works hard to make sure all doctors and nurses working with Abbey are on the same page.

"Our job is to help Abbey *fight*," Katey tells them. "Our job is to help Abbey find any options that can lead her to a whole and healthy life."

The call comes on December 16 at 5:45 a.m. Organs are ready for Abbey. Katey, Scott, and Abbey have three hours and fifteen minutes to arrive at the airport. Miraculously, after leaving Abbey's sisters in the care of family and friends, they make their flight and land in Nebraska an hour later. Abbey is gifted with a new liver, a small bowel, and a pancreas.

They settle in again for a long recovery at the hospital. Doctors tell Katey and Scott to expect Abbey to be there for about six months.

Katey holds Abbey in her arms when the pain is too strong to bear alone. Katey reads the Bible aloud to her. She plays the guitar and does everything within her abilities to help her daughter live, feel comforted, and know she's not alone.

Every day is a roller coaster of extraordinary hope and terrifying fear. The Pool and Spa Safety Act passes. Days are categorized as good or bad to chart Abbey's progress and determine each step of treatment. A good day might mean she has no fever and can eat a few Goldfish crackers or play a game. A bad day might mean she needs an emergency surgery. Fifteen times Katey watches physicians wheel Abbey away into yet another surgery room. For a time the little girl's body complies, and hope builds. Then something fails, and the roller coaster plummets. Abbey bounces back and then is hit with an infection, a bleeding wound, or a high fever.

Katey stabilizes her emotions by reading Scripture, praying, and relying on the army of people who support their family while they help their daughter fight for her life.

Katey rests on Matthew 6:34: "So don't worry about tomorrow, for tomorrow will bring its own worries. Today's trouble is enough for today."

"When we walk in difficult places," she says, "God sends us strength and nourishment to face what comes our way. Not all at once, but day by day." Sometimes Katey and Scott find they need God's strength minute by minute.

Katey just wants to take her little girl home.

In February 2008 Abbey is moved out of the PICU to the pediatric floor. Hope increases. Many tubes are removed. They have a brief respite from the intensity of the PICU. Abbey plays, eats, and speaks up for herself in many situations. These few days in the pediatric unit are a gift and a treasure for Katey. She is able to see Abbey laughing at games of Sorry! and talking with the staff and family. The sound of her voice is a treasure to hear.

On February 19 Abbey's path takes a sharp turn. Doctors put her on a ventilator.

On February 24 she is put in a medically induced coma to help her body recover from a serious infection. Her parents never hear her sweet little voice again.

In early March Abbey's new organs begin to fail. Her body rejects her liver. She needs dialysis to remove excess fluid from her body.

Countless infections and sixteen surgeries. She's been fighting for so long.

"Selfishly," Katey says, "we wanted her to keep fighting for us. We loved being her parents. It is impossible to describe the joy she brought to our hearts."

On March 20, 2008, at 6:10 p.m., beautiful, sassy, independent little Abigail dies quietly and peacefully with her family at her side.

At Abbey's memorial service, I am in awe of Katey's strength. It's not the kind of strength that denies pain but one that openly admits how challenging and difficult life is. Despite the hardships, she clings to hope and still believes life is worth living.

Four years later I see Katey's strength again. The slideshow at the fifth-grade graduation stops on a picture of Abbey, highlighting her little freckles and her happy smile. The gymnasium is quiet as everyone in the room pauses to remember this brave little soul taken too early. Katey cries silently in her seat.

Later, when I speak with her about this time, I hang on to her every word as she describes the beauty of Abbey's life.

Katey says, "As a parent, we always feel like we should be able to fix things. Some things are out of our control, but I can easily blame myself for the events that took place. Why did we have to go to the pool anyway? It was 5:00 p.m. on a Friday, and I thought it would be easier to eat dinner at the pool with friends than to clean house and have people over. I could have just let her keep riding the scooter in the driveway. Then maybe things would have been different."

Katey feels strongly that those nine months she had with Abbey after the accident were a gift. "If Abbey had died that night at the pool, we never would have fully known what a truly amazing girl she was. We were always impressed by how observant she was. She watched everything going on around her and spoke up when she questioned any of it. Before, when Abbey saw people with disabilities or differences, she would comment. Not in a derogatory way—she just noticed everything. But after her injury, Abbey never mentioned any differences. It brought out her heart and her compassion, which was so incredible to witness."

Katey reflects on God's presence through the tragedy. "We were given an opportunity to know who she really was. We loved her before, of course, but over those nine months, we learned Abbey's character. She may have lived a short life on the calendar, but she endured a long lifetime's worth of pain and suffering. And through it all, she brought joy and happiness to every person who knew her.

"I love my children with all my being. Today I try to remind myself daily to be the mom I was before June 29, 2007.

To laugh big, to dance, and to be silly. I have to remind myself because it all can get lost in the broken bits of my heart. Life is a gift, one I never truly understood before our journey with Abbey."

When I asked her if she felt brave during those months, Katey says, "No. I did what every other mother would do. I held it together. I clung to God. I tried to protect everyone as best I could. I never asked why it was happening, but I relied on this verse: 'Surely God is my salvation; I will trust and not be afraid. The LORD, the LORD himself, is my strength and my defense; he has become my salvation' (Isa. 12:2 NIV).

"We miss her so much. But we know that she is now safe. My guess is she's got her hair washed and she's wearing perfect lip gloss, some fancy jewelry, and the most beautiful dress imaginable."

Brave. Beautiful. These words don't even begin to describe the courage it takes to keep on living life and finding joy after such tragic loss. But Katey and my neighbor Zibby (who eventually found out her son died of myocarditis) show us all it is possible when we place our hope in a God who sees us and hurts with us. I don't think for a minute all this pain and brokenness is what God wants for us, but I do know and see through these women that he offers us strength, community, and his gentle hand to help us through.

FOR REFLECTION

1. When enduring a long season of crisis, what beliefs, behaviors, and values emerge as strong enough to endure the loss and grief? If you've never experienced this sort of trial, try to identify the beliefs, behaviors, and values shining through Katey's story.

2. What saddens you most about Katey's experience with Abbey? What about this family's story did you find to be brave or beautiful? What gives you hope in the hardships you are facing right now?

3. The apostle Paul wrote about his ministry in Asia: "We were crushed and overwhelmed beyond our ability to endure, and we thought we would never live through it. In fact, we expected to die. But as a result, we stopped relying on ourselves and learned to rely only on God, who raises the dead" (2 Cor. 1:8–9). How do you know when you've reached the limits of your ability to endure hardship? What does it mean in a practical sense to "rely only on God" to get you through?

4. The author of Hebrews said that we can "run with endurance the race God has set before us. We do this by keeping our eyes on Jesus, the champion who initiates and perfects our faith. Because of the joy awaiting him, he endured the cross, disregarding its shame. Now he is seated in the place of honor beside God's throne" (12:1–2). What race is God asking you to keep running? What people or examples has he placed in your life to help you finish strong?

Eleven

BELIEVING

Define yourself radically as one beloved by God. This is the true self. Every other identity is an illusion.

Brennan Manning, *The Rabbi's Heartbeat*

Since leaving patient care, I now work in marketing and business development for a treatment facility, so I'm not on the front lines of life or death. I do miss patient care. I miss the patients so much, but I take this time to do the healing work I need to do. What exactly that is, I am still unsure, but I am trying to be mindful. I am trying to listen to my body and to God. I am slowing down.

It's hard. I like to run and talk fast. I like things explained quickly. I journal when I pray because I can't sit still in the quiet spaces. I can't think of anything worse than a road trip. Being trapped in a car for long hours requires all the patience in the world.

Therapy and the process of revisiting places deep inside me that I don't want to visit is long and arduous, like a road trip. I am impatient. I want things fixed now. Let's move on! Let's get on with it! I have things to do! I tell my therapist I'm not interested in opening the box of memories and pain that I've closed and locked and stuffed away. I tackled it in therapy once before, wrote a book about it, and moved on. What's the point of revisiting it?

But some of my "stuff" has seeped out of the box without me unlocking it, and despite my own understanding, it continues to affect my life and my thoughts. My eating habits and my body image are in a much better place, but it's the thoughts full of shame and self-loathing that still get me.

I need to pull out the box and open it up again. My therapist says that in order to be whole, I need to embrace all parts of myself. I can't push them away and lock them up in some deep place. I must allow them to be part of me.

"Yeah, yeah," I say. I think her psychology is for the birds. I think I *am* living whole.

Oh, but God in his masterful timing shows me otherwise. Here in the uncomfortable spaces where there are no quick answers and twelve-step plans, I am learning. I have to believe I'll find healing in this process. And I trust this work will lead me to embrace truths I've been running from. Because I had no idea I was running.

It's my forty-third birthday, and I'm having a birthday breakfast with my dad and sister in an adorable little breakfast spot in Kansas.

Most of my life my parents have jokingly referred to me as an accident. Or "the other one." I've believed this story. I know my exorbitant amount of energy and strong will exhausted my family. I know this because I now have a child just like me. He's pretty awesome, though, and we try to celebrate his energy. He can push the bar as far as it will go and can light up a room with his smile. He's also extraordinarily sensitive. Just like me.

So I've accepted this family story, this idea that I was "the accident." It is filed away in my mind under "truth." As the accident, I feel I owe a debt to my family. It's up to me to prove to them not only that I wasn't an accident but also that I deserve to live. Somehow I must pay for all the pain I caused them with my eating disorder and suicide attempt. My beautiful children, my good job, my strong marriage, and my healthy weight are all signposts to show them: *See, I am okay. See, you don't have to regret my existence.*

The problem is, when we live according to others' truth about our lives, when we try to be the people they *think* we should be, we can't become the people God *says* we are.

At the restaurant our full plates of pancakes and sausage come. Someone says something about me being the accident. It's such a common phrase in our family that no one questions it.

But today I feel like questioning. I say, "Dad, you know you've been saying that my entire life. Was I really an accident?"

He looks at me and chuckles. "Oh, Lee. No, you weren't an accident. Since your mom lost her only sibling to cancer, she didn't want to have just two kids. She wanted to have a third just in case something happened to one of you."

I've never heard this story before. Now I'm not the accident; I'm the fill-in child. The backup plan. I joke with him because that's what our family does with pain. We brush it off. My dad means no harm.

"Oh, Dad. You should stick with the accident story. It sounds so much better." We all laugh. I drink my coffee and move on. But inside I'm not laughing. Inside I have this new knowledge. I was the understudy. The "just in case we need a backup."

I also know a person can't live a full life as the understudy. Because what if you're never called onstage? You just stay in the wings, never fully stepping into your star role.

For a long time I have been standing in the wings of the show, waiting to be me, but God is whispering, "This isn't your role. You aren't the understudy. Despite what your parents planned for your life and despite how you think you should be as a person, I have an entirely different show for you. One in which you are the beloved desire of my heart. But you have to step into that role and stop playing the one your parents have put you in."

I think about this and ponder it for a while, then tuck it away in my box.

God has no desire to be tucked away. He reminds me of this so often it's almost comical when I think about it now.

I'm sitting in the chair again, the chair with the threadbare material, staring at my therapist. She has her yellow notepad and her tea. She's calm. I wiggle my leg and try to sit still.

She says, "I am not here to allow you to not be you."

It comes out of nowhere, this strange comment of hers. Or does it?

She continues, "You are always saying, 'Yeah, but …,' and I am not participating in that mission of your life to ignore the difficult parts and only allow the good. All of it is part of your story. You want to not be you. And I will not help you with that."

I argue with her. Yes, I actually argue with her about how I can't be me. Because what I am is the accident, or maybe the backup plan. What does it mean to give up this identity? If I do, then who will I be? It's hard to describe this. It's hard to make sense of it, but that day in the office she identifies exactly the race I've been running and why I'm so tired. Why my body is telling me it can't do it anymore.

God is trying to get my attention, trying to speak his truth into my life. I'm really scared to believe something new. This message of being the accident is one I've bought into for forty-three years. How can I believe anything different?

I start to slide slowly again into old dark thoughts and depression.

So I go away for a silent retreat to one of my favorite places in the world, a place called Pacem in Terris, a retreat center in northern Minnesota. I try to go once a year to get away from the busyness of life and spend quiet time with God and nature. And sleep. Usually when I arrive, I sleep for ten to twelve hours, my body desperately clinging to the rest. Even though I love people and love to talk, I cherish time with God at this beautiful place.

During this particular visit, I want to talk with God about this session with my therapist. I want to work through the pain and try to understand. I've brought the book *Life of the Beloved* by Henri Nouwen with me. And throughout the weekend, this verse continues to pop up in my mind: "Wait patiently for the LORD. Be brave and courageous. Yes, wait patiently for the LORD" (Ps. 27:14).

My season of healing is not a step away from the pain but a step toward it, into it. Daring to stand in it. This takes courage. Bravery is an action, right? Yes, but sometimes an action of waiting. Waiting and asking, "Can I stand in my pain and grow strong in it?"

Yes.

Can you?

"The deep truth is that our human suffering need not be an obstacle to the joy and peace we so desire, but can become, instead, the means to it,"[1] I read in Henri Nouwen's book.

This surprises me. My brokenness can be a gateway to joy. I thought I had to prove I wasn't what my family said—an accident, an understudy. But today, on a path cradled by leaves and a slight touch of sunshine in the quiet woods, I walk slowly and I cry out, allowing my pain to have its place.

I let it cut deep into me. I allow myself to weep about it. I have lived this way for so long, but I now have a choice to believe something entirely different—that God in no way sees me as an accident.

I soak in the words of Nouwen's book. "The sense of being cursed often comes more easily than the sense of being blessed, and we can find enough arguments to feed it."[2]

God knows how much I love books. He knows how often simple words are a balm to my weary soul.

Nouwen wrote, "We are called to claim our unique brokenness, just as we have to claim our unique chosenness and our unique blessedness."[3]

What is this chosenness? What does it mean to believe that our unique blessedness represents what *God* thinks of us?

Later, I sit on the dock, staring out into a quiet pond, and I remember a conversation I had with my friend Julia, a chaplain I used to work with. We were talking about my writing, and I was talking about how crazy I thought it was that God would entrust me with writing a book.

She said, "Of course, Lee. Because he adores you."

I squirmed. "What? Adore?"

She paused and leaned in closer. "Why does that make you so uncomfortable?"

"What?" As if I could pretend that I don't wear every emotion on my face and that she couldn't actually see my reaction.

"Adore!" she said again. "Lee, God *adores* you."

"No, no, no." I tried desperately to change the conversation. Her brown eyes were so soft and kind, and I avoided them. I looked at the door, the ceiling, anywhere but at her.

How does everyone know how to hit me at just the right spot? Or is God teaching me something through them?

"He does, Lee. He does," she whispered.

I believe God loves me. I believe God takes care of me. I believe God goes before me and makes a way for me.

But do I believe God adores me? Do you?

I can't imagine this. Why would he adore me? I can tell you he adores *you*. But me? I am the accident trying to prove my worth. I am running to prove something. But he stands there, looks at me, and says, "No, no. *You* are my beloved. And I adore *you*. Just as you are."

That's honestly the most challenging thing for me to believe. Because I know me. I am messy. I make thousands of mistakes. I am selfish and bossy and hot-tempered. I can believe God adores others, but not me.

But the truth is God adores me. This phrase punctures me deeply. I say, "I am an accident, proving my life." God says, "I adore you."

Which do I want to own?

To believe God adores me despite me is a deeper and richer kind of love than I've ever known. I can't seem to wrap my mind around it. I falsely believe God bases his love for me on my actions. I begin to see I've bought into a lie.

He loves me and adores me, just for me. And he feels the same about you.

This is the essence of wholehearted living. It's birthed out of the love he has for us.

I've spent a great portion of my life trying to be good enough when all the while God is leaning over, whispering into my ear and yours, "I adore you. Don't you see that? I adore you just as you are. Won't you rest in that?"

"Yes," I say in the quiet space of the leaves and the trees. "Yes, Lord Jesus, I am done running. I am done striving. I can't say it will be easy, but I am going to believe that you adore me. I am going to lean into who you say I am. Not who the world says I am."

Will you? This, according to Henri Nouwen, is the deepest affirmation of our true selves.

FOR REFLECTION

1. How does it make you feel when someone suggests that God adores you just as you are right now? What do you say to this idea?

2. What lies do you believe about yourself that you need to let go and let God heal? If you're not sure, ask him to reveal the truth to you about who you are and how he feels about you.

3. What do you think of Nouwen's claim that "the sense of being cursed often comes more easily than the sense of being blessed, and we can find enough arguments to feed it"? What arguments feed your belief that you are bad or unworthy? Write down three arguments for God's love that contradict these.

4. In Romans 5:8 the apostle Paul said, "But God showed his great love for us by sending Christ to die for us while we were still sinners." What do you think this says about the relationship between God's love and our flaws?

Twelve

CHOOSING

The man or woman who is wholly and joyously surrendered to Christ
cannot make a wrong choice. Any choice will be the right one.

A. W. Tozer, *The Set of the Sail*

There are piles of books to my left and right and an overflowing bookshelf behind me. I usually have a few books in my bed with me at all times. So you could say I love books. When I was a teenager, I hid my copies of V. C. Andrews's scandalous books under my white-brass daybed. And when I wasn't devouring those, I was caught up in the latest Choose Your Own Adventure book. These volumes offered me an opportunity to be the one in charge, to be the one who chooses the characters' next steps as well as the ending. At a time in my life when the world felt tremendously out of control, these books offered me a sense of grounding in the mystery and wonder of imaginary stories.

But in real life, when we don't have a Magic 8 Ball or the ability to do anything but trust God to lead us, making choices can be extraordinarily hard. The answers seem evasive when there is no bush bursting into flames, no sea parting in front of us, and there is only God allowing us to be human and exercise our free will in the choosing. It makes me nuts. *God, can't you just give me the answer? Why do you make me guess?*

Nicole never learned Arabic in seminary classes. Egypt wasn't on her radar when she was envisioning a life overseas, but Egypt is where she and her husband are making their home. They're here to learn Arabic and help families start up small businesses. Nicole knows staying isolated in her tiny flat full of brown furniture will only prolong her feelings of loneliness, so she places herself in situations where she can meet people. She walks in a big city full of bustling cars and people busily going through their days. The cool wind blows, a welcome relief from the hot, thick air filled with dust and sand.

A little girl with a worn dress and tattered shoes runs up to Nicole, who's grateful to see a friendly face. Nicole bends down to her level and listens intently, despite not knowing what the little girl is saying. But she can see her deep brown eyes filled with a playful glow. Nicole learns her name is Nadia. Nadia grabs Nicole's hand and pulls her to walk with her.

Nicole holds one finger up to tell the little girl to wait, then runs inside to get her husband. The three of them walk together silently, and Nadia leads them down the windy dirt road to her home.

An act of friendship.

A sign of welcoming.

Being unexpected houseguests is not how they want to make new friends, but Nadia is insistent. The doorman to the apartment building is the girl's father. He wears a long robe called a galabia. The family lives in small concrete living quarters at the base of the building. He listens to his daughter's introductions, then happily takes the couple down to the little apartment filled with large dark furniture and colorful worn rugs. The mother comes to the door with a headscarf draped around her head. Her eyes are full of brightness, like her daughter's.

She embraces Nicole as if she is family.

The mother serves tea, and three other children gather around to gawk at Nicole and her husband. Conversation isn't possible because of the language barrier, but animal noises are, so the little girl snorts like a pig, and Nicole says, "Pig!" Everyone erupts in laughter. When laughing with the family over the universal sounds of pig and goat and dog, Nicole feels like she has come home.

She has prepared for years to work on the mission field, and through the simple kindnesses of tea, laughter, and a little girl's hand, Nicole finally feels settled. She is exactly where she is supposed to be. For her, choosing to live overseas isn't necessarily an act of courage. It's more an act of passion and desire. She knows this is her destiny, her calling.

But on a Sunday morning shortly after meeting Nadia's family, Nicole is thrust into her own choose-your-own-adventure story. She's taking a shower before church when her husband rushes into the bathroom in a panic.

An urgent phone call.

Her mom is on the phone.

Nicole quickly wraps herself in a towel and pauses to look into his face. He looks stricken and worried. Something is terribly wrong.

She listens to her mom's frantic retelling of the story, but she hears only fragments. Father. Heart attack. Arteries blocking the blood's flow.

She learns how the church community sprang into action and how doctors and nurses sitting in the worship service rushed to his side and resuscitated him. She's relieved but scared. Her family needs her now. Her mom says, "Please come home."

I am home, Nicole thinks. *This is home.*

A crushing weight settles into her soul as she realizes she and her husband might have to choose to leave the dream. Leaving so soon, so early in the process, will cut the head off their own plans. They need more time.

How do you choose when both options are good options? When God can use either one?

Nicole wonders how to know what the right decision is.

In another town across the world, Patty is also at a crossroads. How can she know the right thing to do about her marriage?

"Go pack your things," she tells her husband, Kyle. "You aren't staying here." This is the end of her rope. The alcohol called to him again, and he couldn't resist.

"You can't do this to us anymore," she says through sobs. "I can't allow you to be in this house anymore. You can't do this to me. I won't allow it. I won't let our kids see me allowing this."

Kyle is dull-faced and defeated. Stunned, he shows no emotion and blinks. He puts a hand to his face as if she has hit him.

He walks to their bedroom and begins slowly placing his clothing into a duffel bag. Patty stays in the living room, tears streaming down her face while her one-year-old bangs on the plastic tray of his high chair. Her nine-year-old daughter, Emily, runs into the room, waving her arms and crying hysterically.

"Mommy! Daddy told me he's leaving!" Tears soak her sweet face. "He can't leave! Where will he go? How will we do it without him?" Her firstborn is so determined to set things straight, always.

These are all good questions, but Patty has to help her little girl understand that what her father has been doing is not okay. Patty begins picking up toys in the cluttered living room, trying to stay calm, trying to hold back her anger. She doesn't look Emily in the eyes, just says matter-of-factly, "He drank again."

Her six-year-old daughter, Lisa, is now there too, also crying, also looking at her to see what will happen. Patty is at a loss, but this was the plan. Kyle knew the plan. She has to be strong.

"Mom. Please, Mommy, won't you give him another chance?" Emily cries.

She has given him so many.

Patty and Kyle were high school sweethearts who married in college. Kyle joined the US Marines, and they lived in various states before settling in her hometown to begin raising a family. There were no warning signs of the trouble to come, no hints that Kyle might not be able to handle his anxiety or his alcohol consumption. Would she have chosen something different had she known? Would she have flipped the pages back and thought, *No, thanks, not going to do this. This is not the life I planned?*

No.

Because our lives are not like the Choose Your Own Adventure books, and we can't hit reverse.

There were job layoffs for Kyle and promotions for Patty. With a three-year-old and an infant, they agreed one of them needed to stay home. Patty had the job, so Kyle became the stay-at-home parent until he could find work, and then Patty would stay home.

His social circle began to shrink. At the park, moms huddled together, chatting and laughing, and he was left to be the playground supervisor. He felt frustrated, alone, isolated.

He found a secret friend in alcohol. It worked for a while, until it didn't. Patty was pregnant again, and she began to worry because despite her urging, the drinking didn't stop. Instead of counting the days until the child was born, she counted the days of drinking. She prayed the baby came on a day he wasn't drinking. She was relieved to look into Kyle's sober blue eyes, his hands holding hers steady, when she delivered their third child, a son.

She held on to hope that he would stop. On his own.

But she later saw how addiction is a disease. Very few can just stop on their own.

Patty received a slurred phone call from Kyle while he was on his way to pick up their oldest child from preschool. Time moved painfully slowly as Patty jumped into her car and rushed to the preschool, her mind flooding with thoughts of what could happen and questioning how many times he'd done this before. She called him and demanded he stay in the parking lot and wait for her. He waited. When she pulled up, she saw her precious child peering out at her from the truck window, happy to see Mommy. Kyle stood next to the truck, reeking of beer.

She couldn't believe this was her life.

Both women face a choice, and they must choose without any guarantees. Their decision may work out okay. It may not.

Nicole has no idea whether to go home or stay in Egypt. Coming to Egypt felt right. Going home feels right.

She wants nothing more than to run home and be with her family, but her new life is here in the Middle East. They've worked so hard to get here, and so many people have been struggling alongside them in this venture. So many people count on them. Guilt begins to seep into Nicole's every thought.

For days she weighes the options like she's digging through laundry for a certain pair of pants. Picking and sorting, trying to find something to offer her the right answer. Each day her panic rises, gripping her chest tighter. She can no longer breathe in this place she loves. Nor can she imagine going home.

Going home feels like giving up, but staying feels impossible.

Nicole decides she needs to put her family above her mission. She and her husband make arrangements to move back home. They begin to say good-bye to those they've known for only a short time. Even so, she considers them family. Nadia and her parents and siblings, their first friends, are so sad to see them leave. In the weeks leading up to her departure, the land and the people no longer feel the same. Nicole feels like a tourist, an American on a trip to visit a foreign land, and this brings her deep sadness.

Nicole's bravery is in choosing to return to a life that doesn't include her dream for an international ministry. She has no plan, no script for what comes next.

She packs away what she can fit in two suitcases and leaves everything else behind. Nicole and her husband return to the United States with memories and friendships packed tightly in their hearts.

Her dad has quadruple bypass surgery. Nicole helps him during his recovery. She and her husband stay with her in-laws for a while, then move back into their old house, which a friend had occupied for them while they were in Egypt. The same house. The same cars. It's almost as if they never left. As if Egypt were just a fleeting dream.

Nicole struggles with the unknown. So much of her life was planned. Now she's unsure how to proceed. She struggles with fears of inadequacy and failure until she reminds herself of the most valuable lesson she learned in this journey: her life will never look as she imagined, and stepping into the unknown takes more bravery than following a path clearly laid out for us.

Patty knows her husband needs help. She also knows she wants to fight for him, for his recovery, and for their marriage. She challenges him: "Are you just going to keep accepting this choice you continue to make? Or are you going to fight to stay with this family?"

He goes to treatment, and she attends the family groups with him, crying the whole time. The counselor, Troy, asks her to write a letter to his addiction. She can't believe the anger that spews from her. She reads it to Troy and Kyle, crying the whole way through. She is ashamed that this is her life. Kyle says he understands her anger, but he can't believe it's his life either. She sees the financial counselor and signs up for a payment plan so he can stay in treatment. They have to pay out of pocket, but the cost is worth saving him and saving their marriage.

While he's gone, Patty enters the attic to get something. She never goes up there. Kyle usually retrieves anything they need.

Now she knows why. As she makes her way up the stairs, she smells it: the stench of warm beer. Then she flips on the light and sees it: bags and bags and bags of empty bottles and crushed beer cans. She cleans out about twenty bags. She sweeps up the shards of broken glass and bottle caps. She is dazed by the reality of her situation.

Kyle has relapses and setbacks, but eventually he begins to live sober. It takes Patty a while to trust again. She worries and investigates constantly to make sure he isn't drinking. After nine months of sobriety, they move out of the house. The house with the hiding spots. The house that holds the tears of those horrible memories of fear and wondering if they would survive. After all the boxes are taken out, Patty sits alone in the living room and sobs—sobs of gratitude that their life is no longer overwhelmed by hard steps and fearful phone calls.

Days turn to months and months turn to years, and they begin to rebuild their life.

"When I meet people who are going through a similar situation, I wish I knew what to tell them," she says. "My husband didn't quit just because of one thing. It was all of it: every treatment, every group offered him the tools he needed to get better. But he had to choose to use those tools. He had to choose to fight. Recovery is a choice he makes every day. Now he has the tools, a supportive community, and people to help him."

They're still repairing and working toward wholeness as a family, but for now he is sober.

And he is home.

Sometimes the choices set before us are not about right and wrong, good and bad, life and death. We can trust there is a hand on the side of either option, ready to bless us. God is still God, no matter what we choose.

Today Nicole knows that her bravery in leaving Egypt helped her to have courage in many more unknown situations. It has become easier for her to say yes when God calls. And Patty found her bravery in fighting for her husband and their marriage.

I put these two stories together not only because of the difficult decisions both women faced but also because each woman felt shame about her choices. Patty didn't tell many people about her husband's addiction, nor did she involve many in the struggle within the walls of their home. She didn't think people would understand. She thought they would judge her for staying. Nicole believed people would think she was a failure for leaving Egypt. She thought they would say she was a quitter.

And you know what? I think the Enemy loves this little game. This game of shame.

When he makes us feel like we can't share the most broken parts of ourselves with one another, he wins. If I'm afraid of what you might say or think about my choices or decisions, if I believe that you can't understand, I stay alone in my pain. Alone in my decision making. Alone turning the pages of my life. I can only hope the ending isn't a tragedy.

"Never worry alone," John Ortberg wrote in *The Me I Want to Be*. "When anxiety grabs my mind, it is self-perpetuating. Worrisome thoughts reproduce faster than rabbits, so one of the most powerful ways to stop the spiral of worry is simply to disclose my worry to a friend.… The simple act of reassurance from another human being [becomes] a tool of the Spirit to cast out fear—because peace and fear are both contagious."[1]

It's scary to tell someone what is really going on. It's scary to admit we don't have it all figured out. It's scary to acknowledge we are broken and human. But in admitting we are broken, we can hold each other's hands and help each other. Because there is only one who is perfect, one who is whole, and that is God.

God's got this. God's got you. Life can be challenging and tough and brutal, but no matter what choices you make, God will help you through.

And whooee, do I say amen to that!

FOR REFLECTION

1. What do you fear most when it comes to making difficult decisions?

2. Do you believe most of the important life questions you face have a right answer and a wrong answer? Why or why not?

3. How important is avoiding shame when it comes to evaluating your choices? How might it prevent you from inviting trusted friends into your decision-making process?

4. Think about a choice you made that you labeled as wrong or bad at the time. In hindsight, can you identify a positive effect that choice has had on your life today? What are some of the ways God redeems choices we make that are not in our best interest or that hurt others?

Thirteen

BREATHING

A person who never made a mistake never tried anything new.
Albert Einstein

My therapist wants me to learn to breathe. I guffaw the first time she says this. As if I don't already know how to breathe! But no, she explains that she wants me to learn to be in my body and have an ability to calm myself down. She thinks yoga might be a good idea. The form of this particular exercise can give me some tools. I'm skeptical.

More accurately, I am afraid of yoga. Even if my therapist is right, so many barriers hold me back.

The first one is the clothes. What do you wear to yoga? Of course you wear yoga clothes, but I don't have any, and I'm not going to some fancy athletic store to buy some overpriced leggings just to try it. I see women who go to yoga. Their bodies tall and strong, their cores firm, their arms tight and sculpted. They each walk and breathe with an air of confidence that announces, *This is my body and I am whole.*

Maybe I don't have to say it, but I'm not them.

Second, you can't talk during yoga. It's so quiet that talking would be either rude or embarrassing. And speaking of awkward moments, what if during all that stretching and moving you pass gas?

I like to run, to pound the pavement. I grew up working out to Jane Fonda videos, stepping up and down on a box to loud, thumping music. I like to escape and zone out through running and other intense, fast exercises. In yoga you're supposed to be present and mindful, and you're supposed to breathe.

That's the biggest barrier, the breathing. It's so weird listening to others inhale and exhale so loudly. In, out, in, out. When my husband and I were in our first Lamaze class, the instructor asked us to leave because we couldn't handle the breathing. All we could do was break out in preschooler-like giggles. Once we started, neither of us could control the laughing. The silence only cracked us up more.

Really, the breathing is what makes me most hesitant to go to class. If I have to think about it too hard, I'll make a fool of myself.

But I don't have to confess any of this. For a while I rely on another excuse, which is that yoga has roots in Eastern religion. Many people in the church think yoga is anti-Christian. I tell myself my therapist's suggestion is New Agey, so I should ignore it.

Enter my friend Brooke, who teaches Holy Yoga, an increasingly popular form of the exercise. She hands me a brochure and knocks down all my flimsy barriers one by one. She teaches in a church, not some fancy yoga studio, and everyone wears what's comfortable rather than what's trendy. That factor alone makes everything a little bit less intimidating to me. The brochure explains,

> Yoga is a spiritual discipline much like fasting, meditation, and prayer that cannot be owned by one specific religion. While yoga predates Hinduism, Hindus were the first to give yoga a written structure. Yoga postures were originally named in Sanskrit. Holy Yoga teaches their instructors to teach in their native tongues to avoid any confusion or becoming a stumbling block.
>
> Holy Yoga embraces the essential elements of yoga: breath work [I sigh heavily at mention of this], meditation and physical postures. In all of these elements, Christ is the focus of our intention and worship. There are other concepts and traditions that may be part of some yoga practices that are not typically a part of Holy Yoga, such as chanting "OM" or using chakra theory to explain the interplay of the physical and energetic dynamic in the human body.[1]

I don't know what to do about the prospect of passing gas in a quiet house of God, but I decide to give Holy Yoga a try.

Today is the day before Easter. Despite Brooke's reassurances, I still struggle a bit with what to wear. At the back of my closet, I find some stretchy yoga-ish pants from Target that will have to work. My toes aren't painted, so I'll have to wear socks. Who wants to look at unpainted toes? I know, silly thoughts.

I drive to the church where the class is being held. A couple parks next to me, and I get out and follow them. If I walk in with them, everyone will think I'm a regular rather than a first timer. Their yoga mats are rolled up in cute bags thrown over their shoulders. The guy has a slouchy hat and baggy yoga pants. He's a total hipster. The way he walks is already so relaxed. I *so* don't fit in here with my old bleach-stained Target pants, jogging shoes, and some old sports bra. I don't even have a mat.

Never mind. I follow them coolly and try to act like I've done all this before. I sit on the floor without a mat. Brooke lends one to me. *New girl!* I'm the only one in the room who doesn't take off her socks. *New girl!* I think about leaving, about pretending I received a phone call and have to go *now*, but that would be even more awkward. Besides, I'm writing a book about being brave.

My adorable and super-fit friend begins the class. Her Lululemon outfit accents her perfectly sculpted body. Every time we bend over, my pants show my underwear. Classy. I feel like an elephant in a ballet class.

She plays worship music—songs I love. Soon I settle in.

"Take this time," Brooke says. "This is your time, your time with the Lord. Your spiritual practice."

Yes. I can do this. We start slow and ease into various poses, and my body is happy. It likes being stretched, and I can stand on one leg longer than the girl in front of me. I cheer inwardly.

Brooke says, "Yoga is not a competition."

The man behind me begins the heavy breathing. He takes air in and blows it out. Can't he hear how loud he is? I want to giggle, but then I refocus.

My breath. My life from God's breath. God in my breath.

Yes. In and out.

Later, I look up the word *breath* in the Bible. Did you know it appears almost one hundred times? Where have I been, breathing and living and not even paying attention to the glory that's in the miracle of our breath? What divine majesty we can experience when we pay attention to the Holy Spirit's breath in us!

Brooke is right: breathing helps me move. I think of Acts 17:28: "For in him we live and move and exist. As some of your own poets have said, 'We are his offspring.'" The breathing calms me and I start to enjoy the class. A little sliver of light shines right in front of my feet, and I hear the song lyrics, "Holy Spirit, you are welcome here."[2] Yes, Holy Spirit. Breathe. In and out.

While I'm lying on the borrowed mat at the end of the class, my body shaking from the poses and my eyes closed, I breathe and don't care now how loud my breath is. My mind drifts back to a recent session I had with my body-centered trauma therapist.

My face is cradled by the U-shaped pillow of the massage table while the therapist's tender hands massage deep into my tight neck muscles. My eyes are closed.

"How do you feel in your body?" she asks, her hands now massaging my spine.

"I have no idea," I say.

But we both know I am going to that place deep within me, that dark cave of memory where nothing is safe and life is fractured. I've told her about this place. We talk about it often. I trust her with it. I breathe in and out with the memory.

I'm a little girl hiding in a bedroom. Fists pound on the locked bedroom door, and slurred words come from the woman—the grandmother who's supposed to nurture, bake cookies, and give warm, squishy hugs. But this grandma screams, "You are the devil's child! You selfish little brat!" I am all alone. I cry and hold my body tight with my arms gripped around my knees. I sing to myself, a song with no meaning. Just something to drown out the noise of the screaming and the noise in my head.

As I grew, I buried this memory deep and in the process became fractured, which is what happens when we don't bring old memories to light for healing. This particular scene tends to have a grip on me. My therapist and I both know it needs to be released so I can heal.

"Hold the feeling," she says. "And make it vivid in the body. I am holding you; you are not alone."

She keeps her hands on my back, protecting me. Holding me.

"The Spirit of God has made me, and the breath of the Almighty gives me life" (Job 33:4). I think of this verse, and then an old Amy Grant song "Breath of Heaven" plays slowly in my head.

While lying on that table, silently singing "Breath of Heaven," I sense God is there too. Holding me. I don't have to run.

"Feel him holding you," she says. "You can't change the past. But you can change your healing of the past." And her hands rub from my neck to my spine.

God takes me back into the memory. This time I see something else.

I see him next to me, whispering in my ear and rubbing my back. "You are my beloved," he says. "You are not alone; I am here. I am so sorry this is happening to you, my child. But I love you."

He reaches down and places his wounded hand on my heart. "I will never leave you nor forsake you. Never!" he says, looking into my swollen eyes, touching those places so wounded.

Very early in life I found ways to shut out the abusive voices of my past. To tame their taunting. I didn't allow myself to feel emotion, and I sometimes even blocked out sensation. I refused to provide my body with what it needed: food, sleep, honest relationships. I didn't fully live.

Today I am working on being whole again. This means allowing God, the one who made me, to pick up the pieces of me and slowly put them back together. And I am doing this through breathing and through staying in my body. The breathing and staying help me move. They allow my spirit to go into the deep places where the secrets live, into the crevasses of painful wounds that ooze a tar-like blood.

We all have soul injuries that have scabbed over and covered infections. We all have rooms with locked doors barred to God. We give our lives to Christ and he joins us, but he will await our permission to enter those dark caverns too painful for us to revisit alone. And so with the help of a therapist, a pastor, or a body-centered trauma therapist, we can invite God into those places.

The truth is, God wants every part of us to be invaded with his love, his light, his breath. He wants us to live fully, with our minds, bodies, and spirits aligned with his will. He wants to heal us.

And when you finally let him in, listen. Listen close:

"Why didn't you fix it?" I ask.

"Lee, I was there with you, crying with you, holding you."

Dwelling on this memory while lying on the yoga mat, I again imagine Jesus with me as a child in that awful time. I breathe in and out, staying present, trusting he is holding me. I sense the Holy Spirit's breath filling my lungs and running through my bloodstream, doing its healing work. A sacred gift right under— no, right into—my nose. So simple and yet so profound.

Brooke comes over, and with lavender oil on her fingers, she slowly rubs the sign of the cross on my forehead. *Yes.*

Breath of life. Gift of life. In and out, I breathe. I live, I cry, and I heal. *Yes.*

I made it through yoga and will go again for sure. Next time I might even take off my socks.

FOR REFLECTION

1. When God created Adam, "he breathed the breath of life into the man's nostrils, and the man became a living person" (Gen. 2:7). In what ways do you feel more alive when you invite God to breathe on every part of your life, even those parts you've kept protected or hidden?

2. Do you notice your own breathing throughout the day? Is it shallow or deep? Quick or slow? Reduced levels of stress and anxiety are a benefit of conscious deep breathing. What happens to your heart rate and thought patterns when you focus on slowing and deepening your breathing for several minutes?

3. What does it mean to you to breathe spiritually? How is this related to being more closely connected to God?

4. How do you imagine God's breath on you or within you? Is it a sensation? An emotion? A sound? How can the reality of God's breath make you feel braver?

Fourteen

SURRENDERING

*Who knows if perhaps you were made queen
for just such a time as this?*

Esther 4:14

The eighteen-week ultrasound is a big deal for Megan. She prays it will offer her husband, Eric, peace and excitement about becoming a father. Until this point he's been scared. His own childhood was good, but he doesn't feel like it set him up with the preparation he needed. When asked if he's excited about the baby, he only says, "No! I am scared to death! I mean, seriously, who signs up for this parenting thing excitedly? In all things, I want to do well. But I know from working with teenagers that no one thinks their parents knock it out of the park."

Megan and Eric wait in the small ultrasound room. It's dark and chilly, and Megan is on the exam table, her belly exposed and covered in blue gel. Bobbie, the ultrasound tech, is quiet, her eyes focused on the screen while her hand moves the wand slowly over Megan's belly. Images of the baby, their baby, begin to form on the screen. Megan and Eric both crane their necks to see the little image.

Awe fills Eric's voice. "Look! The baby has strong legs. See! A runner for sure." They're silly with excitement. Eric reaches down and grabs Megan's hand. His face is filled with joy and his eyes are wet with tears. *He's in*, she thinks. He's finally as excited as she is.

They stare at the screen, talking about the legs and the arms and making predictions about their baby's future. Bobbie continues typing on her keyboard and clicking buttons as she snaps pictures and takes measurements. Megan wants to stay here all day in this little room with her husband and her baby.

Bobbie leaves the room quietly, returns, takes a few more measurements, then leaves again. They barely notice her, enjoying the sweet time together. They don't want to know the sex. They want only to be reassured the baby is healthy and has a good heartbeat, which the baby does. It sounds strong.

Bobbie is retrieving paper towels to wipe off the gel when she says, "I am sorry your doctor can't be here. He's in a delivery." She begins to slowly wipe the gel away, and the images on the screen disappear.

"That's okay," Megan says, unsure why her doctor would need to be present. "He doesn't need to be here."

"Yes, he does," Bobbie says and turns around to toss the paper towels in the trash.

Megan can't see Bobbie's face, but the words scare her. She pulls down her shirt to cover her belly and sits up on her elbows.

Bobbie says, "I am not at liberty to say much, but the baby's measurements were not what we want to see at this point." Bobbie explains only as much as a technician is permitted.

The lights are still off. Megan thinks the room smells of fear. Tears begin to overtake the joy and silliness of moments ago. Eric stands frozen, unable to process the drastic change. Megan can hear only her thoughts: *I will have a child with disabilities. This will be okay.*

Bobbie says, "Your doctor will be here at one. Go home, gather your thoughts, call people, and write out the questions you have for him."

Megan has no idea what Bobbie is saying. She makes the long walk with Eric through the building and out to their cars, each carrying the heavy weight of the news.

Her mind is numb. Her heart is aching. Megan and Eric arrived separately and go home separately. At a red light Megan sees something out of the corner of her eye. A massive swarm of monarch butterflies surrounds her, flitting all over the concrete jungle like they belong there, around her and her baby. She feels a sense of peace, as if God is telling her, *I am with you.*

That afternoon they return to the clinic to see their doctor, a small man with kind brown eyes. He wastes no time in delivering the news. "The baby isn't developing the way we like to see."

Megan asks, "Aren't all babies unique?"

"Yes, all babies are unique, but each child develops at about the same rate. We need to see that." He sits back a bit in his chair. "Your baby's measurements are significantly off. Fluid is surrounding the major organs, and the limbs are small."

No runner legs, Megan thinks. Her hope is stolen away in an instant, and her mind dashes to a place of fear. She hears him say, "Megan and Eric, the baby most likely will not make it."

The words are like background noise. *It sounds severe*, she thinks, *but they're wrong. What do they know? They don't know what I'm up for. They don't know how strong I am. I'll show them.*

Megan holds a small list in her hand, the questions she wrote on a wrinkled paper. She wants to know how this happened. Is it because she went in a hot tub? Drank a glass of wine? Did she exercise too much? Not enough? Did she take enough vitamins?

"What did I do wrong?" she asks.

The doctor leans forward and puts his hand on her knee. "Megan, you didn't do anything to cause this."

Megan becomes a lab rat. The ensuing days are a dizzying schedule of appointments and tests: blood work, high-level ultrasounds, amniotic fluid testing, genetic and DNA testing. Again and again Megan and Eric are ushered in and out of small sterile rooms with exam tables, doctors, and nurses. Eric is at every appointment, holding Megan's hand, asking questions, trying to navigate this storm. They're soothed by being able to see the baby on the screen again. She grips her growing belly for comfort—her baby is still growing inside. Still a part of her.

One appointment becomes seared in their minds. They're led into a little gray office with soft leather chairs. The doctor is blunt.

"We need to talk about your options," she says.

Megan sinks into the chair. "What do you mean, *my options?*"

The physician says, "It's okay to interrupt the pregnancy." She hands Megan a stack of books and poems about people who "interrupt" their pregnancies.

Staring at the materials, Megan asks, "What do you mean by *interrupt?*"

"You would be terminating the pregnancy." The physician continues to explain how this would be done.

Now angered by the woman's poor choice of words and lack of tact, Megan replies, "So it's not actually something we would be coming back to, right?" She feels fierce. "It's not that you interrupt my pregnancy like you interrupt a movie or a conversation and come back to it, right?"

"That's right."

These are not my options, Megan thinks. *Why is she offering me these options? This is absurd. She's asking me to make a statement about life. About my child's life.*

Megan knows she wants to walk through this struggle. And over and over again they ask her to make a choice. She won't walk around it. For her, a termination of the pregnancy would be a premature termination of the life experience. A too early end of the struggle, of the grief.

She takes the "interruption" materials to be polite, but inside she's angry. Angry that over and over again in the coming days, she continues to have to answer the same question.

"Do you want to interrupt?"

No. The choice is Megan's to make, and she knows she will wait. She will go through the trial. She and Eric will go through this and they will be okay. They discuss and agree they won't miss out on what God has for them during this time.

Megan and Eric spend many nights tossing and turning in their bed. Every day offers more tests and more information. One night Megan sneaks out of bed and walks downstairs to their dark living room. She kneels at the green bench that sits under a large window. The streetlight boldly shines into the room.

She thinks about Abraham and his willingness to give God the ultimate sacrifice, his son Isaac. She thinks of Hannah, who longed desperately for a child, and then after her prayer was answered, she gave her son in service to God at the temple. Megan spreads out her arms, her hands open wide, and says, "God, I give my child up to you. I give you what you have given me, and I am willing to allow whatever is to come. No matter the result."

She thinks of the butterflies surrounding her car. Tears fall on the carpet as her beautiful moment of surrender is also interlaced with great fear.

"God," she whispers through her tears, "if it's a boy, I will name him Isaac. If it's a girl, Hannah."

The next day Megan receives a phone call with more news. The results are in. "The baby girl"—the doctor says this as if the sex is something Megan already knows—"has Turner syndrome, a genetic abnormality found only in girls. A child with Turner syndrome can live and thrive, but your baby won't due to the other symptoms that are present."

Hannah. Her baby now has a name. Hannah is gravely ill.

Every time Megan hears more news, she receives it like a swift slap in the face. She lies on her brown couch again and again, grieving the baby who lives inside her.

Megan numbly drives to Borders bookstore to purchase a copy of her favorite children's book, *Guess How Much I Love You* by Sam McBratney. She had been so excited to give this book to her first child.

As she walks in a daze through the rows of children's books, she collides with a friend from college. Megan's friend is pregnant too and launches into the usual questions: When are you due? How is it going? Megan chooses to tell her about Hannah, that something is wrong and they don't know if Hannah will live. It's the first of many conversations Megan will have with other women. Women with healthy babies.

She buys the book, exhausted from her outing, and inscribes a beautiful note to Eric. She places the ultrasound photo inside the book. Eric weeps when he sees the note and the picture. He is in love with his daughter. His love is a prayer answered.

That evening their doctor comes to their house and sits quietly in a brown leather chair, listening to them, crying with them, and talking with them for nearly three hours. That night he's no longer only their doctor. He becomes their friend.

Megan knows the only way she'll get through this is by the prayers of others holding her up. So she sends out hundreds of announcements bearing Hannah's ultrasound photo and this verse: "Father, I want those you have given me to be with me where I am, and to see my glory, the glory you have given me because you loved me before the creation of the world" (John 17:24 NIV). It encapsulates all she and Eric want for their story, for their daughter, for this season in their lives. Faith is the life preserver they cling to in this season of grief.

Once a week for six weeks, Eric and Megan return to the ultrasound room for dates with their daughter. Sometimes they bring family, and other times it's just the two of them and their doctor. He makes appointments with them after office hours, when the waiting rooms are empty and the staff has gone home because being around other thriving pregnant women is too difficult for Megan.

The excess fluid around Hannah and in her tissue prevents Megan from being able to feel her move, yet she continues to pray that they might just once be able to see her move. One night, on the ultrasound, with the lights dimmed and the soft images rolling in and out of view, Hannah moves. The room fills with tears of grief and joy. Megan cries, "Oh, look at her. My baby girl. She's dancing!"

As time slogs by ever so slowly, Hannah continues to grow and Megan is accosted with constant questions. Joyful women ask "Oh, when are you due?" and "Oh, do you know the sex?"

She hasn't anticipated this part of the journey. She tries to be honest but also respectful. People become very uncomfortable when she tells them about Hannah's condition.

Time plods on in a long wait for what's to come, which is unknown.

There is no script.

Will she miscarry? Will she deliver the baby? Will Hannah live? How will the story unfold?

Megan has no idea. She simply waits.

Only in the safe confines of her pink-tiled shower does Megan let go, the heat of the water caressing her swollen belly. She stands underneath the water and weeps, her hands on her little girl, still alive inside. She cherishes these times alone with her child. Sometimes in the shower she sings, thinking of Mary, the mother of Jesus, blessed among women. Megan feels like Mary when she thinks about bearing a child who will be placed directly into the arms of Jesus. In the midst of her despair, she is able to find mercy and grace.

People offer unsolicited advice. "Hey, you need to go to a healer!" one person says. An elderly woman presses her hands on Megan's belly without asking, then closes her eyes to pray. Megan stands there awkwardly, a stranger touching her and her girl. She knows not to hope Hannah will live, but with so many people saying all these things, she starts to wonder if this crisis is about her. Does she not have enough faith?

The doctors remind Megan that though people with Turner syndrome can live, Hannah will most likely not survive because of the abnormal accumulation of fluid (hydrops fetalis) in many fetal compartments.

In November the cold winter begins. Megan is out for dinner with her family. She's in a booth at a restaurant, wearing black maternity corduroy pants, black shoes, and a red maternity top with an empire waist that ties in the back. Her hair is wistfully pulled back.

She feels pretty.

She feels beautiful, like an expectant pregnant mother. She thinks this is what all the "normal" pregnant women must feel like. It's the first time since receiving the bad news that she has a sliver of hope for a living child.

The next day Megan goes into labor.

In a small hospital room on the maternity ward, sounds of other women giving birth fill the unit. Megan's room is somber. Her husband, parents, sister, doctor, and an amazing and tender nurse stand around her as she gives birth to her first child. Megan looks up at the faces of those supporting her and can see only tears and fear.

They've prepared themselves for an unhealthy-looking baby. But the reality is worse than their expectations. Hannah is tiny, red, and translucent. So full of fluid. No longer living. Megan holds this tiny little girl and gazes down at her, memorizing what she looks like. Megan doesn't want to ever forget.

The room is heavy with tears. Even the doctor is crying deep, heavy sobs. But Megan feels as if God is present. He helps her with the "why" question simply through Hannah's appearance. When she sees how sick Hannah is, Megan is comforted somehow by knowing Hannah wasn't made for this world.

She holds her until they take her away, rolling her out of the hospital room in her bassinet, the wheels clicking gently down the hallway. She regrets only one thing—not kissing her sweet tiny head.

Megan grapples with the question, why do things like this happen?

She asks the question back. Why not? Why can't something like this happen to someone like her? What has she ever done that is good outside of God's grace in her? What has she ever done to exempt her from the human experience of suffering?

The deep sadness pierces her and Eric, but over time the ache softens. She begins to feel honored that God would trust her with such a heavy suffering.

She remembers Mary, who suffered unspeakable pain over the loss of her son. And as she imagines Mary must have done, she begins to thank God, not dismissing the pain or the agony of her empty arms but feeling blessed to have been chosen to usher this sweet little babe straight into the arms of Jesus.

FOR REFLECTION

1. How do you try to make sense of suffering? What have you had to give up to come to a deeper understanding of why God allows painful experiences in the world? What have you gained as you wrestled with the hard questions?

2. What does *surrender* mean to you in the context of your relationship with God? Does the idea of surrender to God make you feel angry, relieved, confused, empowered, sad, thankful, or something else?

3. Think of a time when your dreams or expectations were not just disappointed, but crushed. What has this experience taught you about yourself? About God? About others?

4. In Genesis 22 you can read the full story of Abraham's willingness to surrender Isaac to God. What does this story say to you about the nature and character of God? Do you believe God is trustworthy?

Fifteen

TRUSTING

To believe with certainty, somebody said,
one has to begin by doubting.

Sheldon Vanauken, *A Severe Mercy*

I promised myself as a parent I wouldn't say some of the things my parents said to me as a kid. The phrase I hated most: "Because I said so!" This declaration stops the conversation. It leaves no room for questions and usually demands grudging obedience.

When I was working at the treatment center, the medical director asked the chaplain and me to start a Bible study group for patients. He wanted the sessions to be focused on reading Scripture and offering the patients hope. But as Julia and I got the group under way, we quickly realized what the patients really needed was a safe place where they could ask the hard questions about the pain of life here on earth. They didn't want us to spoon-feed them faith and then tell them to swallow it in dutiful obedience. So in a small room with dim lighting and a Mary Oliver quote on the wall, we invited the patients to explore and ask questions, to air their wounds, and to get support from us.

The result was beautiful. Many of our patients had been hurt by religiosity and church institutions. In our group they were able to share this pain frankly. For many, being able to wrestle with their confusion in a safe place allowed them to slowly begin to trust God again.

I'm baffled when I meet people who don't ask these hard questions, who don't wrestle with God like Jacob did (see Gen. 32:22–30). I don't believe faith means we must simply swallow the Bible and obey it like a teenager whose parents have said, "Because I told you to." God can handle our humanity, our doubts, our ignorance, our pain, and our yearning. Faith asks us to be vulnerable, to be willing to trust God with our lives even when it's hard, and to believe he loves us so much and longs for us to eventually grow into a more mature understanding of his character and ways.

My friend Stacy is a beautiful example of this kind of vulnerable faith.

She stands in the privacy of her bathroom, rotating her fingers around the growing bump in her breast. Stacy has read the little pamphlets in the waiting room of her gynecologist's office. She knows how to spot a lump. She knows when something is not quite right in her breasts.

She also knows cancer. Her thyroid cancer has been in remission for four years, and her bone marrow is actually functioning as it should for the first time in two years. She was ecstatic when she received the news that no more bone marrow biopsies would be needed to match her with a potential donor. After one more infusion a year from now, she'll be fully recovered. She has survived one of the most challenging seasons of her life, which also included a divorce while she was sick. Life as a single mom is finally becoming her new normal.

But this lump, hard and tender, will not go away.

She goes into her regularly scheduled mammogram and draws a picture of the little bump for the radiologist to make sure he knows where to look.

The test comes back clear.

Stacy is relieved and figures she was overreacting.

A month later she looks in the mirror again. Her little bump has grown.

"Can I come back in?" she asks the mammogram clinic. "The lump is getting larger."

"No," the person on the line responds quickly. Clearly this clinic is used to women who constantly call and fret about mystery bumps in their breasts.

Stacy is unyielding: "Something is wrong. It's getting harder. It feels like a brick in my boob!"

"Sorry." The voice is like an automated response. "Insurance covers a mammogram only once a year."

Stacy won't give up. She calls her doctor and pleads to be seen again. The doctor orders a sonogram.

The expression on the radiologist's face—somber, concerned—is something Stacy has seen before. The furrowed brow communicates clearly that something is not right.

He says, "It doesn't look good. You need a biopsy."

"How is this possible?" Stacy demands. "I just had a mammogram here! I'm very confused."

Her doctor reviews the mammogram, and none of the tumors are visible. Stacy undergoes another mammogram on the spot. Again, no tumors show. In her case, mammography simply didn't work.

A biopsy is performed on three solid masses. Three malignancies.

Stacy is furious and terrified. Three to four months have passed since she first spotted the lump. She sits in the tiny consulting room, staring at the blank wall. She's told she has multifocal invasive ductal carcinoma. The cancerous tumors have already started to spread.

"Oh, God, here we go again," she whispers.

To know Stacy is to know Wonder Woman. The two look exactly alike: the long, thick brown hair, the strong legs, the determined green eyes. But Stacy is a wonder in so many other ways. She has a quick wit and fantastic sense of humor. I don't remember Wonder Woman being sassy or, as the old saying goes, full of spit and vinegar. But Stacy is those things and so much more. This helps her and others as she begins another journey with cancer.

The doctor delivers this life-changing news around Thanksgiving. Stacy doesn't want to tell her children, twelve-year-old Brooks and thirteen-year-old Mallory, until she has all the facts about her prognosis. The road to Christmas is packed with tests and procedures that will help determine the best protocol for treating her tumors.

She undergoes innumerable ultrasounds and MRIs. She describes the MRI as feeling "like a thirty-minute headfirst sled ride down a gravel road lined with police sirens. And jackhammers. And preschoolers banging pots and pans."

She feels like she's the dice in a Yahtzee game, thrown into a cup, shaken around, and tossed out again and again. Where will she go today? Which doctors will she see? Which tests will they order? What results will come in? There's no method to the madness. Stacy feels dizzy and at the mercy of the doctors' holiday schedules.

She hides her emotions from her kids. Her fear releases itself in the confines of her shower and throughout the sleepless nights, which she spends pacing the floor of her bedroom.

On Christmas Eve, Stacy meets with the oncologist. They're in a tiny exam room. This doctor with a baby face and a thick head of hair looks fresh out of medical school. She's nervous. Her life is in his hands.

"The growth is more rapid than we originally thought," he says. "We're changing your status from stage two to stage four."

Stacy couldn't be more shocked. She's silent. The doctor writes down everything he says. Stacy just stares at him. Then for two and a half hours, they make decisions about her health. Her future. Her life.

She's frank, as she always is. "I will do anything but chemotherapy!"

He's equally blunt. "Okay," he says. "That's fine. You're in charge of this. But if you don't do chemotherapy, you will not see your children graduate from high school."

The shocking reality of her situation stabs Stacy deeply. Her children. Her son and daughter are everything to her.

He continues, "If you want to survive, you have to have chemotherapy. The cancer is growing too fast. We'll do a PET scan to see if it has spread, and if your PET scan comes back clear, we'll let you do surgery first."

Stacy takes this option. He schedules the PET scan. They must check for brain, spine, and lung cancer because if the cancer has progressed that far, surgery will be a waste of time. She doesn't ask many more questions. She schedules the test. She makes the plans. And when she returns to her car, she cries.

She loses track of time sitting there in the cold parking garage, sobbing in fear. It's time to tell Brooks and Mallory.

The day after Christmas, she and the kids are in their pj's and the house is a typical after-Christmas mess. Stacy calls them down to the living room to talk. She has no idea where to begin. She wants to wear a brave face for them so they won't be scared. It's awkward, this sudden family meeting out of nowhere, the memories of a fun Christmas day so fresh. They each take a post on the big sectional, Stacy in the corner, Mallory in the middle, and Brooks in the other corner.

She says, "I need to talk to you about something, and I don't want you to be scared. We need to talk about this, and Mom might get a little upset, but I don't want to scare you."

She stutters over the words. They're stuck in her throat. "Mom is a little sick."

Brooks and Mallory are only mildly surprised. She's confused until she realizes they think she's referring to her mom, their grandma. She changes gears and says, "No. I am sick."

And she lowers her head and begins to cry.

She feels the fear in the silent room, sees it in her children's frozen expressions. Her precious children.

Mallory breaks the silence, her eyes wide in question. "Is it cancer?"

"Yes," Stacy says. "But a different type than what I had before." She looks into her daughter's innocent blue eyes, now filled with tears.

Brooks asks, "What kind? What kind?"

"Breast cancer," Stacy says.

Brooks sucks in a breath and puts both of his hands on his head. They know enough about breast cancer to think the worst.

Stacy tries to get Mallory to talk, but she just cries.

"We are going to see the best doctors. We are going to be okay. We got through it once, and we will again," Stacy says.

Brooks rushes over to Stacy and wraps his arms around her, his head on her shoulder.

He lifts his head, his face wet with tears. "Mom, I don't want you to go away."

She puts both of her hands on his shoulders and looks deep into his eyes. "I am not going anywhere."

Finally Mallory speaks, her voice like a child's rather than a young woman's. "Mom. Are you going to die?"

"No!" Stacy says.

"Do you promise?" Mallory asks.

"Yes." Stacy swallows her fear and says, "Yes."

Brooks peppers her with more questions. They talk about chemo, surgery, medication, recovery, cells, the risk. He sounds like an adult. Stacy tries to respond appropriately and thoughtfully. She doesn't have all the answers.

She's paralyzed by her own anxiety of not being able to participate in the kids' everyday lives as she does now. She frets over losing her beautiful, thick long hair. *How will I look? Will other kids stare at me and make fun of my children? Will I be able to go to their games?* And again the returning thought, *How will I look?* She says these things to the kids.

Her sweet son says, "Mom. We don't care what you look like. We just want this out of your system."

Brooks leaves to go upstairs. Mallory rests her head in her mother's lap, and Stacy strokes her hair. Both of them cry, trying to comfort each other's deep pain. "I am so sorry," Stacy whispers through her tears. "I'm not sure why this is happening to us again."

"I just want you to be okay, Mom. I just want you to be okay."

Stacy promises over and over while praying, *God, please don't let this be a promise I can't keep.*

Surgery is scheduled for the next week, pending the PET scan results. She'll start with a double mastectomy. Stacy gathers her family and closest friends and gives them clear instructions regarding her children. She says, "They need you all to be strong, positive, and encouraging. They'll need to see humor as well as sadness. They'll need to see fear *and* strength. I want you to give them all the information they ask for. Nothing will be a secret."

Wonder Woman Stacy is ready to fight the cancer. She has only one goal: living so she can be there for her kids. Word of a clear PET scan comes less than twenty-four hours before her scheduled surgery. This is just the way she wants it, without much time to feel stress. The surgeon gives a green light.

She checks into the hospital, dons her flimsy gown, and consults with her doctors. She meets with the pharmacist, the plastic surgeon, the anesthesiologist, the surgeon, and everyone else helping with her surgery. Her IV is inserted, and she rests under a heated blanket.

She's anxious but prepared. She prepared her kids, her house, her workplace, and herself for this battle. She is ready.

Then everything changes.

With minutes to go before surgery, the doctors make a U-turn. Visible tumor growth, swelling, and skin thickening are a new concern. These increase the surgeon's risk of leaving cancer cells behind.

"The final decision rests with you," the surgeon says. "I'll do the surgery, but I advise against it."

Lying there moments from surgery, an IV inserted into her arm and all the other details finalized, Stacy sees her plans come to a screeching halt. She has to decide, but she feels like she can't even breathe. Her head is spinning. She starts to cry. In this mind-numbing moment she wants only one thing: to go home. She starts ripping out tubes and frantically unplugging herself from machines. "I am taking this IV out myself if someone doesn't do it *right now!*" she screams.

Her shocked doctors apologize. One of the nurses begins to cry.

Stacy grieves her dizzying set of circumstances for a few days, then returns from her corner to fight. Sixteen weeks of chemotherapy. Eight treatments.

She's going to lose her hair sooner than she expected. Besides her worries about her children, losing her hair feels like the worst part. "I wish I weren't so vain about it," she says. "But I can own that. I'm worried about how it will affect my kids. I'm trying to be strong about it, but I really hate it."

She has to have all three chemo drugs: two drugs from an IV bag and one the nurse slowly pushes into Stacy's port from a large syringe full of bloodred poison. Stacy stares at the drug called the "red devil," praying it will kill every cancer cell.

She tells the doctors, "Bring it on. Give me two weeks to recoup, and then let's do it again."

In the spaces between the nausea and the needles and the constant ache in her body, Stacy questions God.

Her emotions swing from anger to prayers for healing and peace.

One day she yells at God, "Why me? Are you punishing me?" She doesn't believe he punishes his children, but she is angry. *Why is this happening to my kids again? Why me again?*

Her hope wavers. The strength of her faith depends in part on how she feels from day to day. She hates not feeling 100 percent faith filled that everything is going to work out and that she'll actually find healing. Is her faith in the hands of medicine, or is it in God, who can handle this? She doesn't know. It's a scary place.

"God will only give you what you can handle," someone says in an effort to comfort and help her. The words only hurt her more.

She believes. And she doesn't.

She is human and she is terrified.

She relies on the promise she made to Mallory, the promise not to leave her.

"I hope some good comes out of this," Stacy says to me. "These young girls, my daughter and my daughter's friends who are going to be women soon, I want them to say, 'We watched this good thing happen. We watched her power through and survive.' Because I know with the statistics, they'll all be touched by cancer in some way unless science figures out a cure."

Stacy is strong. And she is vulnerable. And she wishes more than anything she wasn't in this battle. She tries to trust God with the answers to her questions.

"The most terrifying thing right now is that I have to put my life in the hands of some doctor I just met six weeks ago. I have zero knowledge of the science behind cancer treatments, and I've always been someone who tries to be in control. And this—I have no control over this. I am in complete surrender to God's plan."

When I ask her if she feels brave, she tells me, "I am brave. I have to be. In the situation I'm in, I have no other choice than to be brave. Because if I wasn't, I would succumb to much more difficulty than I feel even now. I still have to be the professional, the mom, the friend, the daughter. I have to be the cheerleader at their sports games. I have to cry and rest and feel the way I feel. And all that takes bravery. Because the truth is, I don't feel good. I don't look normal. I'm losing my hair. All this takes bravery, but it also takes strength to just decide, am I going to move forward or am I going to let it define me?"

She finishes, "I will *not* be defined by cancer. It doesn't make sense to me."

As I write this, Stacy's latest CT and bone scans have returned with no sign of metastasized cancer. The tumors didn't respond to the chemo as well as her doctors hoped. Evidence of living, aggressive cancer cells in them persist. But with the reduction of affected lymph nodes, the chance of it spreading is also reduced. Stacy has hope.

She continues to question and trust God in the process. I find this kind of faith beautiful. God can handle Stacy's questions, just as he handled Jacob's. God can handle yours.

The staff writers at Got Questions Ministries offer this insight into Jacob's story and ours: "What we learn from this remarkable incident in the life of Jacob is that our lives are never meant to be easy. This is especially true when we take it upon ourselves to wrestle with God and His will for our lives. We also learn that as Christians, despite our trials and tribulations, our strivings in this life are never devoid of God's presence, and His blessing inevitably follows the struggle, which can sometimes be messy and chaotic. Real growth experiences always involve struggle and pain."[1]

FOR REFLECTION

1. What does it mean to you to trust God? Describe how you demonstrate your trust in him in practical ways.

2. What situation in your life right now is testing your confidence in God's goodness or love for you? What factors or circumstances cause you to question him or make it hard for you to trust him?

3. Proverbs 3:5 says, "Trust in the LORD with all your heart; do not depend on your own understanding." How might your understanding of God or of life get in the way of the good he wants to accomplish in and through you? How might the tension between

what you believe and what you don't understand help draw you closer to God?

4. Have you ever emerged from a difficult season of your life feeling as though your faith in God is stronger than it was before the struggle? How would you describe this transformation to someone who wants to know how such a thing can be possible?

Sixteen

RISING

*Never give up then, for that's just the place
and time that the tide'll turn.*

Harriet Beecher Stowe, *Oldtown Folks*

When I was a child, Christmas was wonderful and awful at the same time. On Christmas morning we opened gifts, hugged, and laughed together as a family. But almost invariably, the week that followed went south. If I wasn't "good" or if I didn't "behave," I would often hear, "You better be nice, or I am going to take those presents away" or "All the time and money we spent on you, and this is how you act?"

So it might come as no surprise to you that upon receiving any sort of gift, whether it be friendship or time or even a listening ear, I feel indebted to the giver. I feel obligated to live up to the value of the gift.

When I left my job at the eating disorder treatment center, the staff sent me off with a really generous going-away party. I attended with a mixture of feelings that ranged from gratitude to sadness, but the overwhelming emotion was embarrassment. Who feels embarrassed at her own send-off?

I do, apparently. It's not as though I planned to feel that way, but I did.

The going-away party was full of people I loved—people with whom I had worked, grieved, laughed, and experienced life. Working with patients who are near death is not like any other job; you get to know your coworkers extremely well. Doctors, nurses, dieticians, and therapists gathered to celebrate *me*. I was horribly uncomfortable. I sipped way more wine than I needed and talked rapidly, trying to make everyone else feel comfortable.

One of my therapist friends, Ryan, noticed my discomfort and asked, "Lee, why is this so hard for you?"

I didn't have to reach too deep to find the answer. "I feel like I owe everyone," I told him. "Everyone is so nice and kind to me. I feel like I owe you something."

In 1995 depression and an eating disorder sent me to the dungeons of a dark pit I couldn't claw my way out of. The momentary pain and darkness were unlike anything I can describe. I believed my only option—despite my faith, despite my love for my boyfriend and my family—was to take my own life.

By the grace of God I received the gift of a second chance at life.

Because of this gift, Deuteronomy 30:19 became my life verse: "Today I have given you the choice between life and death, between blessings and curses. Now I call on heaven and earth to witness the choice you make. Oh, that you would choose life, so that you and your descendants might live!"

I had tried to take my own life, but God had other plans. He offered me this choice: would I continue to do the things I had been doing, which were obviously destroying me, or would I reach out, put my hand in his, and walk forward into the life he had for me?

I chose life that day. A young twenty-three-year-old me, full of depression and fear and truckloads of self-loathing, picked life. I decided to step into the game and trust that God wanted me alive more than my depression wanted me dead.

This experience of mine isn't party conversation or dinner conversation. Talking about wanting to die, about the ache and depression deep in our souls, isn't even church conversation. Because we all know we're supposed to trust God, right? We all know we must have faith.

This is what I believed at the time. So what did I do about it? I decided to trust hard enough. To have enough faith. To do enough good to live up to the gift God and others had extended to me. I would prove I was worth keeping alive. I would show everyone that my life after the suicide attempt could be better than it was before.

In other words, not only would I prove to my family that I wasn't an accident, that I was more than a backup plan, but I would also repay my debt of life.

Twenty years passed. Twenty years after my suicide attempt and my decision to make amends, I was exhausted. I was in the wilderness, and I was scared because all this time I thought I owed God and the world. All this striving to make amends for my mistakes was killing me all over again. I had thought my job at the treatment center was the cause—and maybe it was in part—but the bigger culprit was all this trying and striving.

Because the truth is, people don't like to talk about pain. These stories I've shared in this book—sometimes people don't want to hear them. They're too hard. Too sad.

Oh, friends. To think we don't face this choice between life and death every day is denial. We *need* to talk about this. This is why we need a Savior and why we need one another. Real life is hard stuff.

But I am not afraid of it, nor should you be, because when together we shine a light on the darkness that can so easily swallow us, we can escape it. Then we can rise.

Stephanie has been following her calling to teach in the church but has had a challenging time working out the details. As she likes to say, "I've had some good moments and some downright failures."

But then a pastor invites her to preach at his church. She hasn't stepped onto a stage to teach for about eight months. This time when she stands up to preach, she doesn't put on the mask of teacher, which she has often donned in the past. She doesn't set out to impress anyone or even to do a great job. Instead, she immerses herself in the text, listens to God, and shares from her heart. She speaks to the congregation simply as Stephanie.

It's the first time she has ever stepped onto a stage without feeling like she's stepping into a competition. Everything about it is a redemptive experience.

I'm sitting in this small auditorium, and what Stephanie has to say is a gift to me as well.

She focuses on Elijah and says, "Elijah had just reached a point of burnout. He was doing lots of things for God but not getting the outcomes he hoped for. God wasn't meeting his expectations and Elijah ran away, done with it all. 'But he himself went a day's journey into the wilderness, and came and sat down under a broom tree. And he prayed that he might die, and said, "It is enough! Now, LORD, take my life"' (1 Kings 19:4 NKJV)."

Clearly I wasn't the first person to feel this way, although when I was in it, it seemed as if I was desperately alone. But Elijah felt this way too and that encourages me. Many of the women I've interviewed for this book have felt this way, lost in the wilderness and afraid, thinking, *It is enough, Lord! Take my life! Please!*

But Elijah also said, "For I am no better than my fathers!" (v. 4 NKJV). What did he mean by this? I believe he was worn out from striving, from competing, from trying to *do* instead of *be*. I believe he was exhausted from trying to excel, from comparing himself to those who had gone before him.

Stephanie says, "When Elijah is so worn out, he runs away. He runs to the wilderness. A place where we have been and where we are going. The question is, do you stay in that place? Do you make the in-between place your forever place?"

She continues, "The wilderness is a place where we can hear God's voice. Wilderness is where God speaks to us about who we have been and who we are becoming."

I'm listening to this sermon only a few weeks after my going-away party. I hear the sermon on the heels of the twentieth anniversary of my second chance at life. I absorb Stephanie's words and know I'm at a crossroads. I'm not sure what the next steps are, but I know I need to let go of the idea that the purpose of my life is to redeem the pain I caused others and let go of the idea that I owe something to my parents and this world that would justify my existence. That's my wilderness place, and it's not the place I want to stay.

Where we think there's a period marking the end of our life, God places a semicolon. The semicolon is that funny punctuation mark with a period stacked on top of a comma. It's a mark that connects two complete but related ideas. It's a pause, not a stop. It says, "Hey, wait—this idea isn't finished yet."

In that semicolon God tells us there is more to come. So much more.

What do you do when you are at a crossroads? I implore you to do what Elijah did—pray.

I pray.

And I sense God saying, "We are in a new chapter, Lee! A new place of living. You don't need to prove anything. Just trust in me. Rest in my arms."

Did you know there's a trend of people getting semicolon tattoos? When I started looking into this, I learned the symbol is popular among people who have struggled with depression, suicide, addiction, or self-injury. The semicolon tattoo is a symbol of strength, a reminder of how the self can overcome.

I'm not sure I like all of that definition, so I made up my own. In my mind the semicolon doesn't represent the power of *me* but the power of God. I look at it and am reminded that my struggles never mark the end, that God never leaves us in the wilderness, and that this verse is true: "'For I know the plans I have for you,' declares the LORD, 'plans to prosper you and not to harm you, plans to give you hope and a future'" (Jer. 29:11 NIV).

Stephanie continues and this is my favorite part: "In the Genesis account, God calls the day *tov*, which means 'good.'"

Stephanie says, "God calls things good not just when they are grand and beautiful but when they are partnering with him in the act of creating. Trees are good not just when they are full-grown trees or just when they bear fruit but also when they produce seeds. *Tov* is in each of us as we partner with God to make this place more beautiful, more wonderful and loving. *Tov* is a seed, not a result. It is not our job to be better. This is not a competition. We are called to bring our *tov* into the world; we are called to be ourselves."

As Elijah slept under that broom tree,

an angel touched him, and said to him, "Arise and eat." Then he looked, and there by his head was a cake baked on coals, and a jar of water. So he ate and drank, and lay down again. And the angel of the LORD came back the second time, and touched him, and said, "Arise and eat, because the journey is too great for you." So he arose, and ate and drank; and he went in the strength of that food forty days and forty nights as far as Horeb, the mountain of God. (1 Kings 19:5–8 NKJV).

God told Elijah to arise and eat. If he'd been providing for me, I'm sure God would have laid out by my head a Costco cake with *lots* of white frosting, and a huge glass of Diet Coke.

Stephanie points out, "God doesn't chastise. He doesn't shame him. God comes alongside him and brings him food to eat!"

Do you notice he took a nap two times? Elijah was knocked out. He napped, then ate, then napped, then ate again. God took care of the details.

We don't need to scramble to make ourselves worthy. Remember, God adores us even when we're in the wilderness and just need to take a nap.

"But please note," Stephanie says, "Elijah doesn't stay in the wilderness. It is okay to be in it, to rest and be fed, but then we need to rise up! And eat!"[1]

Where does our food come from? Besides Costco cakes, God provides us spiritual food in the form of people. I don't draw this from

Elijah's story as much as from my own experience. What has sustained me and nourished me these last twenty years? People. People who have come alongside me, who know me and accept me just as I am. Many, many times God has sent a message to me in the form of a fellow human being. He gives us what we need to feed one another.

After this interlude, Elijah knew God had seen him. He understood that God knew everything about him, even that he wanted to die, and God still loved him and took great care of him.

God sees you. God feels your pain. God hears your joy. He will provide the rest and sustenance you need because he loves you right where you are, even in your wilderness place.

There is still more to my story and there is to yours as well. When we put a period and think it is the end, God puts a semicolon. So I decide to personalize this symbol. I walk into a tattoo shop and get a semicolon tattoo—a symbol of my own to remind me that my story isn't over yet. God is still at work.

I am learning this is true in my own life. I don't have to strive to be enough. Because of God's great love, I *am* enough. And so are you, brave, beautiful woman. You are seen. You are known.

In *Pooh's Grand Adventure*, Christopher Robin poignantly tells Winnie-the-Pooh, "There's something you must remember…. you're braver than you believe, and stronger than you seem, and smarter than you think."[2]

I believe God says this about us too.

Fear not. You cannot outrun God's grace. Only a risen God can gift us with all this. So rise up from your wilderness rest and go forth in your beautiful bravery.

FOR REFLECTION

1. When you receive a gift, do you feel obligated to the giver, or can you accept the gift freely? What do you think the reason is for your attitude toward gifts, whether they are physical or spiritual?

2. Do you believe God's gifts of salvation and grace come with obligations or with strings attached? How would you describe the difference between dutifully obeying God and joyfully responding to God's love?

3. What event or crisis has led you to cry out, "Enough!"? What signs of hope do you see that these circumstances might not be the period marking the end of your life? What more might God have planned for you? If you can't see anything, ask God to show you. Ask the people he's placed in your life what they see.

4. Have you run to a wilderness place for a season of rest? What do you think God is prompting you to do there now? Rest? Eat? Rise up and go?

Seventeen

CHEERING

*Deep friendship is a calling forth of each other's chosenness
and a mutual affirmation of being precious in God's eyes.*
Henri Nouwen, *Life of the Beloved*

As I was writing this book, I felt a lot of doubt and fear. I kept asking myself, what if life is only about keeping your head above water when you feel like you're drowning? What if this is it—this struggle, this constant battle to survive? You see, the process of writing down the stories for you has stirred me up inside. I have more questions, new fears. Will I be the mom burying her child someday? Will I be the woman with the lump? Will I be sitting next to my husband, admitting him for treatment?

I've been eating a lot of mac and cheese and hot dogs and drinking more wine than I need. It's a way to avoid the fears that sometimes overtake me. Sometimes I scream in my sleep, calling out for 911 or longing for someone to comfort me. Are these terrors from my own wounds? Or have I become too entrenched in these women's stories? Probably a bit of both.

This world is scary. Some people make very bad choices that have far-reaching effects. More often we make *good* choices, but that doesn't exempt us from cancer and death and hardship and pain.

I have to confess: this reality makes me angry. But what makes me even madder are people who say stupid things about difficult circumstances. When I was deep in my depression, someone said, "Just let go and let God!" Or another doozy: "Can't you see how great your life is? How can you be depressed?" There were people who told Megan that she needed to pray more for baby Hannah's healing; people who told Katey that God had a plan in her daughter's horrible suffering; well-meaning Christians who told Alison that she actually did need to continue obeying her parents, even though she had long been a parent herself.

When my anger passes, I remember I've been like these people. I have said similar things. Aren't we all on this journey together, just trying to figure it out?

I sit in therapy and learn I have work to do. I have my own wounds that still need healing, but I don't resist any longer. I don't resist because I have a new courage imparted to me by the women featured in this book, who have taught me so much.

As I said in the beginning, none of us walks through this life without a story to tell or wounds to be healed. The truth is, life is really tough, and it is full of challenges. Every time I see Katey, I marvel at how she is still getting out of bed every day after losing her baby girl. Some days *I* hardly want to get out of bed, and I haven't been through half of what these women have gone through. I am working through my story, though, as they are working through theirs.

We don't have all the answers. But are we supposed to? Not always. Instead, we trust.

That's the choice we make in living every day in this unpredictable place called Earth. The question I want to pose to you now, at the end of the book, is this: are you going to live alone or with others in authentic, loving community?

One day I hear my friend Nancy ask, "Who is cheering for me?" She's been up all night asking this question with tears falling down her face. Her husband sleeps next to her, resting for the marathon he plans to run the next day. She'll be present, cheering him on. But she holds this question in her mind, wondering.

"Who is cheering for me?"

My heart aches when I hear her say this because I want to reassure her. I want to mend her heartache. I am cheering for you! I think you are amazing. I think you are kind and tenderhearted, and you are such a great mom. I admire the passion you show your children.

I want to tell her these things. I want her to know how big an impact she makes on her world just by being herself. That while she runs another car pool or puts in another load of laundry or washes another dish, we—the women who know and love her— are cheering for her. And I do tell her these things, over and over.

What we often miss in this world of social media highlights and swiftly moving news feeds is that we desperately need one another. Each of us needs a cheering section. I need a cheering section.

I also tell her I'm sometimes jealous because she doesn't have to work outside the home. She tells me her jealousies, and we laugh at how we each think the other has it better.

Jealousy robs us of community and togetherness. Envy is a barrier between us. It keeps us isolated. It keeps us alone. I find myself getting caught up in it so often. *Why can't I do what she's doing? Why can't I have what she has? Why can't my life be as easy as hers?*

When I planned to write this book, I thought I'd have to ask around and put out a search party to find brave women whose stories would be worth reading. Because when I look around me, I see women with beautiful clothing and perfect bodies and awesome accessories. I see their perfect houses and their apparently easy lives, and I think for sure they have it all together.

It turned out I didn't have to do an *American Idol*–like search for women who've been through the wringer and survived. I didn't have to hunt for beautiful bravery. These women, all of them, were right in front of me. They come from the neighborhood where I live, the office where I work, the church where I attend, the grocery store where I shop. They come from my childhood.

I believe you know such women too.

The notion that anyone's life is easy is a mirage. It isn't real. To imagine any of us is without pain and suffering is to deny what it's like to truly live in this world. Conversely, denying or diminishing our own pain by comparing it to someone else's is equally unhelpful. *I shouldn't feel so sad (or depressed, anxious, hurt, upset)—so-and-so has it so much worse than I do.* While it's good to adopt a healthy perspective on your own suffering, another person's agony isn't the cure for yours.

We need to drop the act, quit pretending we have it all together. Because we don't. We are *all* merely stumbling along this path of life, trying to do the best we can to live well. We're not all stumbling (or walking or running or limping or sitting) at exactly the same point on the path, but we are all on this journey together.

So can't we be a cheering section for one another? Instead of saying, "Oh, I want what you have," which separates us, we can say, "You go, girl!" Let's hold up signs and let's encourage one another. When one of us is beaming with joy and happy news, let's holler and cheer and give bear hugs. When one of us has collapsed at the side of the road, we can rush to help, saying, "What do you need? How can I come support you?"

Women, we are one another's cheering section! We can hurt, but we can also heal—in community, living closely. That's how I believe God intended for us to live.

"We do not want merely to *see* beauty," C. S. Lewis wrote. "We want something else which can hardly be put into words—to be united with the beauty we see, to pass into it, to receive it into ourselves, to bathe in it, to become part of it."[1]

The stories I've recorded on the previous pages aren't tied up neatly in pretty little bows, because this side of heaven is hard. I want these stories to pose the hard questions about how we perceive our pain and how we can bravely press through it. Sometimes the nice pat answers we learned in Sunday school about obeying God and trusting him aren't enough. They're true answers, yes, but what do they really *mean*? Faith doesn't come when we have all the right answers but when we offer our questions to God. Even the faith that feels shaky and angry, like Stacy's, is still faith. If we can lean into the ache of the process, if we can dig deep, we will eventually hit water in the well of faith. Then we can take a long drink.

My friend Megan—Hannah's mom, who now has three beautiful kids—summed it up perfectly after reading this manuscript. "The kind of bravery you are talking about isn't the kind that conquers," she wrote to me. "It's the kind that submits and relinquishes control to God. This is true bravery. It is letting our guard down and becoming naked, just like we were always meant to be. Trusting God and relying on him, just as he made us to do.

"When we suffer like these women have, like Jesus did, we become more like him only when we surrender to him," Megan said. "When we choose to believe that God can take care of us best, that he is in our breath, this is when bravery shines and we can grow in faith and in community. Then we can release our burdens to his care and the compassion of others. That's the only way we can get through this struggle. When he is all we have, and when he shows us himself through the dear friends he's given us, we are shown the only way to live—bravely and beautifully."

In this messy life, we need one another. More than anything, friends, we need to stop the games, the gossip, the comparing, and remember that everyone is fighting a battle—you just might not know about it. Satan loves when we can't really see one another. He knows that if he tricks us into believing lies about one another or sucks us into jealousy, we'll never want to be intimately known. But when we draw close to one another and really listen, trying to understand and not rushing to fix, we can participate more fully in the raw, messy, awful, beautiful thing called living.

Be vulnerable. Be real. Be raw and let your naked bravery shine bright. In doing so, you help others see hope. You help others have faith. That is brave. That is beautiful. Now go forth and be that for one another, you brave and beautiful women!

FOR REFLECTION

1. Think of a woman you've kept your distance from because you perceive her to have a better life or circumstance than yours. How might you get to know her? Are you willing to take the risk of reaching out to her in friendship? Why or why not?

2. Who has cheered you on through a difficult time? How did his or her role in your life affect your perception about your suffering and your relationship with God? What good examples from this person's behavior can you apply to your relationships with others?

3. When you need help, are you able to ask for it? What stops you? Do you think it's okay for you to feel negative emotions about hardships, or do you think you must "suck it up" and deal with problems on your own? How have the stories in this book influenced your thinking about this?

4. Think of someone you've helped through a difficult time. Though you might have been in the position of offering support, in what ways did the relationship enrich your own life?

ACKNOWLEDGMENTS

Thank you to all the women in this book, who trusted me to hold their stories. I am so honored. I want to also acknowledge all the brave women whose stories I didn't tell in this book. It's my hope you will be encouraged to share your stories with others in the warm comfort of a safe relationship. May you begin to look for and see the beauty in one another.

And with that, I can't help but thank the tribe of people who held me up with prayer, friendship, encouragement, and funny emojis and texts as I wrote this book. Thank you first and foremost to Dorothy Greco, who was kind enough to introduce me to Alice Crider at David C Cook. Thank you, Alice, for believing in an unknown writer like me and taking a risk on this book! Alongside Alice came the fantastic, amazing editor Erin Healy. People, this book was shaped and molded by the graceful guidance Erin so courageously gave me! What a blessing she has been. Thank you also, Shannon Ethridge, for taking me under your southern wing.

Thank you to my friends who are such beautiful, brave women: Julie Greene, for letting me escape to your cabin and for the many late-night phone calls with me whining about what a horrible writer I am; Janna Northrup and Wendy Padgett, for always reading everything I send you and giving me such invaluable feedback and friendship; Marta and Caroline, for allowing me to pop in and out of the writing group; my dear friend Heather, for the miles of runs and therapy. What a gift you are. And to my "texties" group: special thanks for the constant prayers, laughter, wine, and friendship. I love you all.

Thank you to the Redbud Writers Guild. What an amazing group of beautiful writers. I feel blessed to be included.

Thank you to my therapist, who so expertly guides a chaotic me. Thank you, Tove, for helping me release the pain in my body.

Thanks to my sister, Kristin, for always encouraging me. And thank you to thirteen-year-old Megan Carver, who came up with the idea for how to break up each chapter in this book. You are an amazing young woman and I am so grateful for you.

Thank you to my husband, Chris, and my beautifully brave boys, Matthew, Michael, and Tommy, for letting me hide out in my office so much. I love you all. You buoy me. You fill up my love tank. You keep me going.

Most of all, thank you, Jesus, for your unending grace and the love you offer us all.

NOTES

CHAPTER 2: CONFRONTING

1. "The War on Women's Bodies," National Eating Disorders Association, www.nationaleatingdisorders.org/war-womens-bodies.

2. C. S. Lewis, *The Lion, the Witch and the Wardrobe* (New York: HarperCollins, 1950), 39.

3. Brené Brown, *The Gifts of Imperfection: Let Go of Who You Think You're Supposed to Be and Embrace Who You Are* (Center City, MN: Hazelden, 2010), 26.

CHAPTER 3: SHIFTING

1. Henri J. M. Nouwen, *The Inner Voice of Love: A Journey Through Anguish to Freedom* Image Books ed. (New York: Doubleday, 1998), 72.

2. Henry Cloud and John Townsend, *Safe People: How to Find Relationships That Are Good for You and Avoid Those That Aren't* (Grand Rapids, MI: Zondervan, 1995), 67.

CHAPTER 4: TELLING

1. Bessel van der Kolk, *The Body Keeps the Score: Brain, Mind, and Body in the Healing of Trauma* (New York: Penguin, 2014), 96–97.

2. van der Kolk, *Body Keeps the Score*, 79.

CHAPTER 5: HOPING

1. David Wilcox, "Hold It Up to the Light," *Big Horizon,* © 1994 A&M Records.

2. Rick Warren, interview by Paul Bradshaw.

3. James H. Olthuis, *The Beautiful Risk: A New Psychology of Loving and Being Loved* (Eugene, OR: Wipf and Stock, 2006), 199.

CHAPTER 6: REINVENTING

1. Ruth Haley Barton, *Strengthening the Soul of Your Leadership: Seeking God in the Crucible of Ministry* (Downers Grove, IL: InterVarsity Press, 2008), 22.

2. Hillsong United, "Oceans (Where Feet May Fail)," *Zion,* © Hillsong Music Australia, 2013.

CHAPTER 7: FORGIVING

1. Nadia Bolz-Weber, *Pastrix: The Cranky, Beautiful Faith of a Sinner and Saint* (New York: Jericho Books, 2013), 148.

2. Nadia Bolz-Weber, "An Evening with Nadia Bolz-Weber" (lecture, Festival of Faith and Writing, Calvin College, Grand Rapids, MI, April 16, 2016).

CHAPTER 8: SEPARATING

1. Felicia Snell, email message to author, May 7, 2016. Used with permission.

2. Elan Golomb, *Trapped in the Mirror: Adult Children of Narcissists in Their Struggle for Self* (New York: William Morrow, 1992), 28.

CHAPTER 11: BELIEVING

1. Henri J. M. Nouwen, *Life of the Beloved: Spiritual Living in a Secular World* (New York: Crossroad, 1992), 77.

2. Nouwen, *Life of the Beloved,* 61.

3. Nouwen, *Life of the Beloved,* 71.

CHAPTER 12: CHOOSING

1. John Ortberg, *The Me I Want to Be: Becoming God's Best Version of You* (Grand Rapids, MI: Zondervan, 2010), 122.

CHAPTER 13: BREATHING

1. "What We Believe," Holy Yoga, accessed June 28, 2016, https://holyyoga.net /about/what-we-believe.

2. Jesus Culture, "Holy Spirit (feat. Kim Walker-Smith) [Live]," *Live from New York,* © 2012 Sparrow Records.

CHAPTER 15: TRUSTING

1. "What Is the Meaning of Jacob Wrestling with God?," GotQuestions.org, accessed August 3, 2016, www.gotquestions.org/Jacob-wrestling-with-God .html.

CHAPTER 16: RISING

1. Paraphrased from Stephanie Spencer, "Arise and Eat" (sermon, Genesis Covenant Church, St. Louis Park, MN, August 9, 2015), www.genesiscov .org/sundays/sermons/media-item/83/arise-and-eat.

2. *Pooh's Grand Adventure: The Search for Christopher Robin,* directed by Karl Geurs (Disney, 1997), DVD.

CHAPTER 17: CHEERING

1. C. S. Lewis, "The Weight of Glory," in *The Weight of Glory and Other Addresses* (New York: HarperCollins, 2001), 42–43.

ABOUT THE AUTHOR

Everyone wants to be perfect, but no one wants to be around perfect. Lee spent most of her life trying to be the "perfect" person the world told her she should be, while destroying her body, mind, and relationships in the process. A deep depression and life-threatening eating disorder led her to dark nights where she began the brave journey to become the woman God designed her to be. She tells her story in her first book, a memoir called *Table in the Darkness: A Healing Journey Through an Eating Disorder.*

Lee continues to bring hope to others through her work as a mental health practitioner in the field of eating disorders and chemical dependency. An inspirational firecracker, she travels all over the country for speaking engagements, where she encourages women and trains pastors, teachers, and leaders in a variety of topics centered around mental health, body image, and cultivating bravery.

Lee's writing has appeared in *Christianity Today* and *Huffington Post*, and she is also a member of the Redbud Writers Guild. She lives with her adventurous husband and three wild boys in Minnesota.

To learn more about Lee, visit www.leewolfeblum.com.